The Reminiscences of Commander Albert K. Murray
U.S. Naval Reserve (Retired)

Interviewed by
Dr. John T. Mason, Jr.

U.S. Naval Institute • Annapolis, Maryland
Copyright ©1994

Preface

During his lifetime, Commander Albert K. Murray did not release the transcript of his oral history interviews. Murray was a superb artist and also talented as a storyteller and observer. He has provided candid recollections of a number of the Navy's top-ranking officers from World War II, along with his explanations of the artistic method used to paint portraits of those individuals. Near the end of his life, Murray befriended the Gilliland family, which was a fortuitous circumstance, because the family is seeing that the legacy of Murray's work is properly preserved. The executor of his estate is Dr. Marion C. Gilliland, who has authorized the release of the oral history transcript. Her mother, Mrs. Marion S. Gilliland, has written the biographical summary included in this volume. Professor Herbert Gilliland of the Naval Academy has also made contributions to the completion of this volume of oral history.

The initiator of this series on Commander Murray was Dr. John T. Mason, who conducted the interviews while serving as director of the Naval Institute's oral history program. Regrettably, Murray's reluctance to release these transcripts was apparently matched by his reluctance to participate in further interviews. Given the degree of insight he provides on a number of his portrait subjects, one wishes that he had discussed many other of his subjects as well. In the interviews, Murray barely touched upon his role as a combat artist in World War II and on his fine series of paintings connected with the light cruiser Boise. In those cases, the excellent art will have to speak for itself because of the absence of amplifying commentary in the oral history. Even so, he has given us some fascinating insights into the processes that went into producing portraits of some of the top flag officers of the Navy and Marine Corps during and after World War II.

Thanks go to Gail Munro of Navy Combat Art, James Cheevers of the Naval Academy Museum, and Barbara Broadhurst for providing a number of the pictures of Murray's paintings that appear in this volume. The inclusion of the artwork enhances the reader's understanding of the images Murray described.

Paul Stillwell
Director, History Division
U.S. Naval Institute
August 1994

ALBERT KETCHAM MURRAY

Painting the blue Mediterranean from the beautiful south coast of France is not normally thought of as a hazardous undertaking, yet it was there that Albert Murray nearly lost his life. Seated on a rooftop overlooking the Mediterranean during World War II, he was caught between German and Allied fire. When the shells began bursting close enough to blast the food off the plates of the troops having lunch around him he decided to pack up his brushes and watercolors and retreat to a safer location. As he stooped to retrieve some of his gear a stray shell clipped the dog tags from the chain around his neck. That was just one of several close calls he experienced during his days as a combat artist.

Born in Emporia, Kansas, December 29, 1906, Mr. Murray studied at Cornell University and the College of Fine Arts, Syracuse University, where he received a Bachelor of Fine Arts cum laude. He was also a fine amateur athlete, lettering in two sports, soccer and the rowing crew.

He furthered his studies of art in England and France and later under the tutelage of the noted portrait painter Wayman E. Adams in New York and Mexico. By 1930 he was exhibiting his works in such prestigious shows as the Carnegie Institute International and the Corcoran Gallery of Art Biennial.

Upon receiving a commission as a lieutenant, United States Navy Reserves in March 1942, he served on a convoy escort in the

Atlantic and Caribbean. Six months later he was reassigned to the Navy's newly created art program and to painting portraits of the Navy's General Board.

He was later attached to the Fourth Fleet in the South Atlantic, where he produced a large number of watercolors showing naval activities in the British West Indies, Brazil, and Puerto Rico. He was later reassigned to the Eighth Fleet in the Mediterranean, where he manned combat stations and sketched incessantly. This duty took him ashore in the assault wave that hit the southern coast of France in the summer of 1944. It was there he nearly lost his life. He also went ashore with the Marine assault waves on the beaches of Italy. He also served in the Pacific theater. For his valor under fire, he was awarded the Bronze Star.

After the war Murray was assigned to paint many of the official portraits of the great men who had led and fought to win the war at sea. Among his major works was a full length, life portrait of fleet Admiral Chester W. Nimitz shown signing the Japanese surrender instrument for the United States aboard the USS Missouri. In the background are Admiral William Halsey and General Douglas MacArthur. Along with many of his other paintings, this hangs permanently in the Pentagon.

For several years after World War II Murray served as Director of the Navy Combat Art Collection. In this capacity, he was responsible for Operation Palette, an immensely successful series of Navy art exhibits that traveled throughout the United States.

Murray's paintings have been shown in many important exhibitions including "Naval Portraits" which included 12 of his works, "Your Navy" at the Metropolitan Museum of Art, "American War Paintings" at the Paris Marine Salon, and "Men Who Made Washington" at the National Gallery of Art. His paintings were shown in a combat art exhibit in the Naval Academy Museum in 1945, and in 1984 the Naval Academy Museum hosted a one-man show of his watercolors, charcoals, and oil portraits of Naval leaders. He is represented in the permanent collections of the National Gallery of Art, the National Portrait Gallery, the National Museum of American Art, and in the Departments of Commerce, Treasury, and Justice as well as the Department of Defense. In 1978 he received the Navy's Meritorious Public Service Award, and in 1982, he was honored further with the Navy's Distinguished Public Service Award.

In his civilian career, he has painted individuals such as Alfred P. Sloan for New York's Memorial Hospital, Rush Kress for the Kress Foundation, Laurence Rockefeller for the New York Zoological Society, Arthur Ochs Sulzberger for The New York Times, and Thomas J. Watson for the International Business Machines Corporation, as well as Oppenheimer of the DeBeers Diamond Company in Johannesburg, South Africa. For several decades he also painted the Secretaries of the Navy, Chiefs of Naval Operations, and Commandants of both the U.S. Marine Corps and the U.S. Coast Guard.

Someone once said that saying that Albert Murray was an artist was like saying that Babe Ruth was a baseball player or that Abraham Lincoln worked for the government. He played in the big leagues and painted America's heavyweights, military and civilian. The biggest names in industry and government reported to his New York studio to sit for their portraits. Several of them considered him their "personal shrink." They felt comfortable with him and they let down their hair, making it possible for him to capture facets of their personalities that more formal relationships would not permit.

He was a perfectionist who would not release a painting until every detail met the high standards he set for himself. He was commissioned to paint James V. Forrestal, first Secretary of Defense, in his Pentagon office. He would not begin until he was assured that the sittings would be uninterrupted, a situation that did not last very long, however. When the portrait was nearly finished it was knocked from the easel resulting in a three cornered tear on Forrestal's collarbone. It could have been repaired, and later was, so that it did not show, but Murray was not satisfied to submit a damaged painting. Forrestal, on his advice, readily agreed to sit for a second portrait.

Aside from his time as a combat artist, his watercolors were reserved for pastime pursuits. He never traveled without a small kit of watercolor materials, a busman's holiday strictly for his own enjoyment. None were ever marketed.

His professional career spanned 65 years. He always felt fortunate to spend his life doing something he loved and rejoiced that he would never have to retire. He died in Gainesville, Florida, March 24, 1992, at the age of 85.

By Marion S. Gilliland
Gainesville, Florida

AUTHORIZATION

The U. S. Naval Institute is hereby authorized to make available to individuals, libraries, and other repositories of its choosing the transcripts of four oral history interviews concerning the life and career of the late Albert K. Murray, USNR (Ret.). The Interviews were recorded by Commander Murray on 29 September 1980, 1 December 1980, 12 January 1981, and 28 July 1988 in collaboration with Dr. John T. Mason for the U. S. Naval Institute.

The undersigned does hereby release and assign to the U. S. Naval Institute all right, title, restrictions, and interest in the interviews. This authorization is given in consideration of the U. S. Naval Institute agreement to permit the estate of Albert I. Murray and the trustees Marion C. Gilliland, Ph. D., and Wendel E. Dreve to use the tapes in any form, whether oral or written transcript form, for projects on or about Mr. Murray's life and career both now and at any future date. This includes, but is not limited to video tape reproduction, written form, or oral use. The copyright in both the oral and transcribed versions shall be the sole property of the U. S. Naval Institute. The tape recordings of the interviews are and will remain the property of the U. S. Naval Institute

Signed and sealed this ___16th___ day of ___July___ 1993.

_____
Marion C. Gilliland, Ph.D.
Executix, Albert K. Murray Estate

9665 Young America Road
Adamsville, Ohio 43802

Phone: (614) 796-4797 Fax:# (614) 796-4799

A. K. Murray #1 - 1

Interview Number 1 with Commander Albert K. Murray,
U.S. Naval Reserve (Retired)

Place: Commander Murray's residence in New York City

Date: Monday, 29 September 1980

Interviewer: John T. Mason, Jr.

Q: I am delighted that at last we are going to sit down with a tape recorder and get some of your wonderful memories of some of these men whom you have painted and whom you have known so well. I think you want to begin by talking about Admiral Halsey.*

Commander Murray: I think some things there might be of interest. The comments that I will be making here are somewhat homey kinds of things, observations of a painter about a man he is painting, and the circumstances.

Q: Observations of that sort, let me say, are rather unique and quite different from ordinary observations.

Commander Murray: They would be different from the book studies and looking at his record, so to speak, on the printed page or something else. I am talking about living with these people. What life is like in their homes and

---

*Fleet Admiral William F. Halsey, Jr., USN.

how I would evaluate them as people. As a painter of portraits, I don't presume to be any kind of clairvoyant, but since I have done that my entire life, I might be sometimes a little more perceptive about certain things than somebody who wasn't so homed in on it, because he didn't have to be. For me, I have to be, and that is part of the problem of separating the wheat from the chaff.

These things were significant and interesting to me, which perhaps could find their way into the portrait itself--maybe a twinkle in an eye or a few crows' feet here or there, or some other kinds of aspects that might indicate a sense of humor for somebody who would normally be thought to be extremely tough and austere. I will come to this with somebody like Admiral King, who announced in the press when he was going to be CNO and said, "I want to tell you fellows [I am not quoting him, but this is only from memory] there has to be a son-of-a-bitch around, and I am just putting it on record that that is going to be me while I am in this job."*

Q: And that's the role he intended to essay.

Commander Murray: What I am trying to say at this point--the man was immensely sensitive and human at the same time.

---

*Fleet Admiral Ernest J. King, USN, was Chief of Naval Operations and Commander in Chief U.S. Fleet during World War II.

He had a gentle streak about him which might be lost with so many of his colleagues. Perhaps some of those going back to his midshipmen days might have been aware of it, or maybe some other who would see it in certain other streaks. All I'm trying to say is that these remarks I will now make will deal with as many facets of the person that I can think of.

Now, back to Halsey. I was asked to paint a portrait of him at a time when he was living down in Charlottesville, Virginia, spearheading a fund-raising business for the university there.

Q: Approximately what year was that?

Commander Murray: I think it was probably about '46 or '47. As you well know, he was a five-star admiral, which meant that he would draw full pay and have a staff with him for the rest of his life. The reason he was down there was that he had spent his freshman year there; he couldn't get into the Naval Academy right away.* He went to the University of Virginia and was a freshman there. After the war, the trustees had started this enormous fund-raising effort for $28 million, which was a staggering sum for that time. They wanted somebody of much distinction to spearhead it, and somebody came up with the idea that,

---
*Halsey entered the Naval Academy in 1900, then graduated in 1904.

A. K. Murray #1 - 4

"Admiral Halsey is an alumnus; let's get him to do it." So that's how he was down there doing it; they gave him a house, and I went down there and stayed in the house with him.

He was enjoying his job down there. He didn't look at all the way I wanted him to look when I was trying to do this portrait, which was at the time of the Philippine Sea campaign, when I thought that Halsey's role was probably as significant as any in his long and colorful career.*

Q: You had seen him at that time, had you?

Commander Murray: I had seen him off and on through the war; I was not present at the Philippine Sea campaign itself, but I am referring to that, because my mission there at the University of Virginia was to make this significant painting--hopefully significant--of the admiral.

Q: Was this under the aegis of the Navy?

Commander Murray: Yes, we were to do a pictorial record of the principal leadership in the naval services (which would include the Marine Corps) of World War II, so we started

---

*The U.S. invasion and reconquest of the Philippine Islands in the autumn of 1944.

with the five-star people and then went on down to significant enlisted types so that we got outstanding performance right straight through without discrimination of top-heavy rank. We broke it down after we got through the five-star people, with ship types, so we would have an outstanding battleship, destroyer, submarine, cruiser, right down the line--and then in the enlisted ranks those who had outstandingly distinguished themselves. This would include the Marine Corps as well as the Navy, so that we would now have a pictorial record of individuals who had brought real distinction to the naval services.

Halsey comes in under the five-star group. As I said, he was not in a mood for me to try to do with him something representing the heat of the war at perhaps one of the greatest climaxes when the fortunes of war hung by a thread there, when the Japs went back to the Surigao Strait in the Philippine Sea campaign. The Japs had this marvelous strategy of coming down through the San Bernardino Strait and the Surigao Strait and nipping off our capacity there by draining away our main support with this decoy which unfortunately Admiral Halsey bit, but much to the objections of his carrier task force commander, Admiral Mitscher, and Admiral Mitscher's chief of staff, Arleigh Burke.* I think the Jap ships were sunk 300 miles away.

---

*Vice Admiral Marc A. Mitscher, USN, Commander Task Force 38 in Admiral Halsey's Third Fleet; Commodore Arleigh A. Burke, USN, was Mitscher's chief of staff.

On the beach were a quarter of a million men under General MacArthur, and left to keep the back door closed from the sea was Admiral Kinkaid, who had practically nothing left to keep the door closed except some old AKs and a few obsolete ships short of ammunition and other vessels.* Halsey took the main strength away on this decoy, because the Japs had made it appear there that they had a massive impending air assault.

Our people, other than Halsey, concluded it was not possible for the Japs to launch a major air assault in this way, because they just didn't have it. We had destroyed it too successfully for them to be reasonably capable of doing it, but Admiral Halsey wouldn't buy it. All the way out, Admiral Mitscher was begging him to turn around, but Halsey wasn't going to be deterred. So when they finally got there, they discovered the truth of the matter--that many of these aircraft were simply propped up by 2x4s and everything else on the flight deck in a simulated takeoff condition ready for a strike, but they were incapable of flight, and they had neither the aircraft nor the personnel to launch it. By this time it was too late and Kinkaid was left in his underwear, so to speak, for a defensive position, back in the Philippines. And at the same time the Japs came down through Surigao and San Bernardino

---

*General Douglas MacArthur, USA, Supreme Commander, Allied Forces, Southwest Pacific Area; Vice Admiral Thomas C. Kinkaid, USN, Commander U.S. Seventh Fleet.

A. K. Murray #1 - 7

Straits but with Oldendorf in Surigao decimating that thing was magnificent, the success and skill . . ."*

Q: With all the old battleships.**

Commander Murray: Yes, but they were practically out of ammunition after they crossed the T there, I guess.

Q: Yes, it was the last time for this classic arrangement for naval warfare.

Commander Murray: Incidentally, in painting Admiral Oldendorf, he was commenting to me about his irritation. When he came back after that--as you may recall that episode, those contacts were just prior to or just after 11:00 P.M. at night, and the whole action took place at that late hour. In first light of dawn he was coming back to report to his boss, Admiral Kinkaid, what he did. As he was coming aboard, going ashore was a whole batch of the press establishment--AP, UP, and everybody else--so with some banter, they said, "What are you doing here, Admiral Oldendorf?"***

---
*Rear Admiral Jesse B. Oldendorf, USN, who commanded the Bombardment and Fire Support Group at Leyte Gulf.
**The battleships involved in the Battle of Surigao Strait on the night of 24-25 October were the California (BB-44), Maryland (BB-46), Mississippi (BB-41), Pennsylvania (BB-38), Tennessee (BB-43), and West Virginia (BB-48).
***AP--Associated Press; UP--United Press.

And he said, "I have come to report to my boss what we did last night."

"Oh," they said, "Don't bother, we have already told him."

"How in the hell do you know?" he said. "I'm just coming in, you weren't with me last night."

"Oh no, we didn't have to be; we just guessed what you did. Probably by the time you get through with him, it will be on the streets in the USA." I don't blame Admiral Oldendorf for being highly annoyed at the press on this issue, but anyway he went on and told Admiral Kinkaid what had happened that night before, which was a brilliant achievement down in Surigao Strait.

Now, back to Admiral Halsey . . .

Q: By the time he got to Virginia, he had shed his armor as a warrior.

Commander Murray: Yes, and he was enjoying his peacetime role very much. It seemed to me, of all the jobs he had had in other commitments--I should get him on board a carrier first of all, because his major role in World War II, although he got his wings in his 50s, and was a very senior officer at the time, I would get him seaborne in a carrier. And to sober him up I tried various things;

Fleet Admiral William F. Halsey

Fletcher Pratt had written a few articles that irritated him a whole lot.* I brought those up, trying to sober him up as he was in uniform in front of me now, and I had simulated a flight deck scene. He is on the bridge in front of the talking tube, and in the air in the distance are some aircraft, so it appears that he is seaborne, and here are these aircraft which identify probably the ship he is on as being a carrier, but I can't get him sobered up here.

Q: This is actually in his home where this is taking place?

Commander Murray: I had a little studio cooked up down there. We were simply living in his home and doing the painting in this makeshift studio. But I got nowhere with one salvo after another trying to get his whole mood turned around to meet my requirements.

Q: Did he fully understand your objectives?

Commander Murray: I didn't want to tell him that. You learn a few little techniques; if you ask somebody to smile as against telling them a joke that makes them smile, in one case it may be forced, and in the other one is a

---
*Fletcher Pratt was a naval analyst who frequently wrote for the popular press of the period.

natural thing. Often they are as different as night from day. I wanted this to happen, not to be made by direction. I wanted to have him irritated, and I finally uncorked this business on the Surigao Strait because *The Saturday Evening Post*, which was then publishing, had two issues, one on Halsey's position and the following week was Kinkaid's.* They were at great odds, and there were tremendous professional, vitriolic exchanges between the two on this issue. So I brought that up, and at this point, he said, "Say, you are trying to get me annoyed, aren't you?"

I said, "Yes, I am." And then I told him, "I want you sobered up here, and I want this thing to look convincing as to the time frame that this painting is presumably representing. That is why I would be delighted to hear any thoughts that might not have been in that *Saturday Evening Post* article that you wrote or other comments in regard to it. I have had a full-length description of this from Admiral Kinkaid. Perhaps I should have told you first, because it makes this one more significant." Let me close up the business here with Halsey in spite of the Kinkaid version which predicates the sharp division between the two men.

---

*Fleet Admiral William F. Halsey, USN, with Lieutenant Commander J. Bryan, III, USNR, "Admiral Halsey Tells His Story" (Part 7 of 9), *The Saturday Evening Post*, 26 July 1947, pp. 26, 63 ff. Admiral Kinkaid's position was presented in Gilbert Cant, "Bull's Run: Was Halsey Right at Leyte Gulf?" *Life*, 24 November 1947, pp. 73-78 ff.

A. K. Murray #1 - 11

Halsey explained all about his position, why he thought there was some validity to the decoy and why he was determined to do it and why he took with him sufficient weaponry to demolish it if he encountered it. He went through his whole repertoire on this thing in about 20 minutes.

Q: Did his anger mount as he went?

Commander Murray: Yes, well he really didn't get very irritated; he did sober up. And those big, bushy eyebrows of his knitted a few times, and it gave me a little different look than what I had been accustomed to seeing there for several days. But I would love to have had it prolonged so that I could really hang onto it for a while.

Then, after about 20 minutes, he said, "Now what do you want to talk about?" The sun had come back out; the storm clouds had disappeared, and now I was back at gate one where I was in trouble in the first place. I had to draw on memory; I did take a few pictures, hoping they might be helpful, but unfortunately they weren't worth a darn. So now I was doing more research on Halsey trying to find other episodes that could help in this same problem.

Q: What did you come up with?

Commander Murray: I didn't, I had to draw on memory for the most part. I encountered a lot of interesting episodes, though, living in the house with him. Mrs. Halsey was an inveterate talker; the moment she woke up she was pressed to start talking about something. She would be on the phone or something else before she had gotten out of bed, and she would be going right straight through until the time to retire again. That used to upset the admiral, because I would wait at the house until I heard from him as to whether he had gotten his desk cleared up so I could go down and get started painting. And she would be on the phone and he couldn't get on. He would send his aide up with a message. He wasn't very polite about it, "Tell Mrs. Halsey to get the so-and-so off that telephone," and the aide, of course, would dress it all up very nicely and convey the message. Come cocktail hour, she would do most of the talking, and one time she said, "Did I ever tell you," turning to me, "about never discount the power of a woman in the Navy?"

The admiral said, "Oh for God's sake, Frannie, don't tell him that one."

That was all she needed, so she started off, just the three of us, and the story went like this: It had to do with the late earning of his wings in the Navy at Pensacola. It seems that at that time there was a junket to go to Iceland; we needed a base up there badly and right away, and there was a mission headed by a certain captain in the Navy that Admiral King wanted, but the Halseys had another candidate that they were terribly anxious to have go. At this point, let me remind the uninitiated that Admiral King and Halsey were very close.

They were good friends in Naval Academy days, and before he had married Mrs. Halsey, Admiral King had had quite a fancy about her himself. And, as I am sure you know, Admiral King had a great fancy for the ladies anyway. So he was always very fond of Mrs. Halsey.

By the way, the Bull Halsey business was unheard of in that house or in the family. The admiral among his intimates was always known as Billy and nothing else. This Bull Halsey stuff was great for public relations, but it was totally unknown in the family and never used by them either, nor by his colleagues and classmates like Admiral King.*

Now, back to this business--they were going to have a big party down there in Pensacola to celebrate the admiral getting his wings, and they invited Admiral King down. The Halseys had cooked up an opportunity to use this to get that captain they wanted to head this junket, apropos Mrs. Halsey's story about "don't discount the power of a woman in the Navy." The script that she and her husband had rigged up went like this: it was a beautiful moonlight

---
*King was in the Naval Academy class of 1901, three years ahead of Halsey.

A. K. Murray #1 - 14

night and a dress affair. She was in a very décolleté evening gown, and when she thought the time was right, she would ask Admiral King if he wouldn't like to have a little stroll in the garden, on this moonlight evening.

Q: A dangerous thing!

Commander Murray: Yes, but that was part of the scheme. So, when she thought the time was right, she asked him, and he was delighted. He accepted with such alacrity that she thought well maybe she better help the situation out a little, so she went by the bar again before they went out and as soon as they were out there, she said, "You know Ernest, Billy and I are terribly anxious to have Captain So-and-so go on that."

"Oh my gosh, Frannie, don't bring that up."

And she said, "Well, I have to, this is so important to us."

"All right," he said, "I'll write some orders for him, but he is not my idea. You know that, but I don't have older friends in the Navy than you two, so I'll write some orders for him tomorrow."

"Oh, Ernest, that's so nice, but you don't have to." She reached in her bosom and pulled out a document, and she said, "Here is a set of orders we had made up for you."

"Good," he said, "turn around." So she turned around, and using her bare back, he pulled out his fountain pen and signed them. He started to fold them up, and he was going to slip them in to his pocket, and she said, "No Ernest, I'll take them," and down the bosom they went again. Very shortly, she disappeared.

We next pick up Admiral King looking around for Admiral Halsey. When he found him, he said, "Say, where's Frannie?"

"What's the matter?" says Admiral Halsey.

"Never mind, let's find her. I've got to see her. Something is bothering me. Come on, help me find her." Knowing what had happened, Admiral Halsey took Admiral King everywhere but to the right place, so they search around and don't find her.

The next morning at breakfast, Admiral King said, "You know, I don't like what happened last night. I want those orders back," addressing himself to Mrs. Halsey.

And she said, "Oh, Ernest, I don't have them. Last night we had a little plane out on the strip all warmed up, and after you signed them, as soon as the ink was dry, they were on their way and are probably passed over the captain's desk at BuNav."*

"Well," he said, "I've never dishonored my signature before, but I'm going to do it now. I think this is

---
*BuNav--the Bureau of Navigation was the organization then in charge of writing officers' orders for the Navy.

outright fraudulent. I don't like any part of it." So the breakfast sort of terminated with indigestion for all of them, but before he left the premises he had a little change of heart. He said, "All right, I guess you are about my oldest friends, and though I don't like any part of this whole thing, I'll let it go this time; but don't ever do anything like that again."

So, with a big smile she said, "See, don't ever discount the power of a woman in the Navy."

Q: Can I guess the name of the captain who got the job?

Commander Murray: I don't recall his name.

Q: Dan Gallery was there.*

Commander Murray: Well, we would have to look that one up. That part of the story was not imparted to me. It was the ebb and flow of these other things that were the fascinating part. Admiral King was very good to certain of his old cronies, and one of them was Jonas Ingram.

Jonas Ingram was running the fleet down in Recife, Brazil, when I was there.** Ingram was a great football

---

*Rear Admiral Daniel V. Gallery, Jr., USN (Ret.), whose oral history is included in the Naval Institute collection.
**Vice Admiral Jonas H. Ingram, USN, Commander South Atlantic Force during World War II.

player at the academy, and he was a great friend of Admiral King. The admiral's friends were well taken care of by the admiral, and in this case I was flabbergasted when I came aboard a houseboat practically to do this portrait drawing of Admiral Ingram down there during the war. This was when we were ferrying great quantities across the hump there at Pernambuco, Brazil, and across the South Atlantic.

Q: By way of Ascension Island.

Commander Murray: Yes, and that was one reason for having a strong arm down there in Brazil, which was Jonas Ingram's command. It was this houseboat episode that got me.

Having had some time before in the Combat Art Section when I was on the inshore patrol, which would comprise anything that could float practically that they could put armament on--anybody's yacht and practically even a dinghy, because we didn't have anything for our antisubmarine activity, and we were operating out of Port Everglades which is now part of Fort Lauderdale. Sinkings by the U-boats were covering all the beaches with oil down there. They would take houseboats or anything else, and the Mississippi was loaded with pleasure craft coming down to the various navy yards and having weaponry put on and depth charges if they were capable and machine gun mounts and what-have-you.

But, lo and behold, down there in Recife was this houseboat that had come down the Mississippi too and then floated all the way down there to Brazil, because that is what Jonas Ingram wanted, and Admiral King was going to get him one, so there it was. So that is what it's worth in regard to Admiral King and a comical episode while I was there with Jonas Ingram--one of his favorites in the Navy was gunnery. I was tagging along with him during this portrait episode down there when he was inspecting a destroyer in his command. This was one of the old types with a gun mount up forward.

Q: A four-stacker?

Commander Murray: No, it wasn't a four-stacker, but it was just after those. At any rate, he climbed aboard this with great restraint, which was ignored by the gunnery officer. The gunnery officer tried to get the captain of the destroyer to get the admiral not to do this, but Ingram was determined to climb aboard the pointer's seat which is like a plowshare on farm equipment, and he started to crank the barrel around when something didn't feel right. He put his hand down around under this plowshare seat and touched it and then looked at his hand, and sure enough it was all covered with fresh gray paint.

The whole gun mount had just been painted, and that is

Vice Admiral Jonas H. Ingram

what the gunnery officer was trying to tell the captain so the captain would keep the admiral from getting aboard the thing. Then when Jonas Ingram discovered that his pants were now covered with this gray paint from the gun mount seat, he was furious. It seems that this was the first time he had this suit on after it came out of the box from Brooks Brothers; it had just arrived down there in Brazil, and now the bottom of it was all covered with this paint. He was fit to be tied. The captain was fiery red from embarrassment, and the gunnery officer was the only fellow in the clear, trying to get his boss to intercede to keep the big boss out of trouble but to no avail. This is just a little homey touch. The rest of us had to turn away to keep from laughing, because this was really a comical episode. But these comical episodes occurred many times.

To digress one more moment, at Salerno we had a staging area there for the southern France operation, which was to be performed by the 36th, the 3rd, and 45th Divisions. They were all being trained on the beach at Salerno. It was a marvelous sandy area, but it had a lot of submerged sand dunes along this beach area; the beach had been heavily mined in training exercises.

We had a terrific briefing going on for the southern France operation. Whole sections of the beach where the assaults would be made were in facsimiles of the beach on tables with every telegraph pole, fire hydrant, and building, and tree and everything from aerial reconnaissance now manufactured in reality so that when the troops hit the beach, they would be looking at something they had seen day after day. And they knew where to look for snipers and this, that, and the other things so they wouldn't come in cold on this thing. They were brought in day after day on this to brief everybody in their sector of whatever beach--red, yellow or whatever--to know what was there.

Q: Were these clay models that were made?

Commander Murray: All kinds of stuff, they used papier-maché and clay and this, that, and the other thing. They were very skillfully made and very convincing; the trees looked like trees and the buildings looked like the particular kind of building they were supposed to be and the streets and the windows and everything else.

Q: Quite a job.

Commander Murray: Yes, it was, but a very practical, useful one, to minimize casualties and increase effectiveness. Then they were having a dress rehearsal, bringing the troops in to the beach in LCIs; that's a landing craft vessel with two ramps up forward. They would drive the thing up onto the beach and drop anchor there so they could pull themselves off, then lower these ramps. Each LCI had the capacity of carrying about 150 men, an infantry company.

On one of the first ones, all the brass was there, General Bradley, Patch, and Patton; a whole crowd of them were there.* Unfortunately the weather had created sort of a small lagoon just before you got to the real beach, so that the LCI couldn't quite get over that first sand dune. So when they dropped their ramps down, they were into that sand dune, but there was still some water to go through before they got onto the beach, and that water was about five feet deep at its deepest part, but it was good sandy beach. So they backed off and tried to come in again but without any better success. So they let the ramps down. The comical part, the reason I'm bringing this thing up now--I had been down on the beach painting a scene down there: some artillery practices going on and also a demolition crew taking the barbed wire revetments out. This was a training exercise for everybody using that beach, when they bring these bangalore tubes of dynamite in to breach the barbed wire barricades that the Germans had put up. That's what I was down there for.

---
*Lieutenant General Omar N. Bradley, USA, Commanding General, U.S. First Army; Lieutenant General Alexander M. Patch, USA, Commanding General, U.S. Seventh Army; Lieutenant General George S. Patton, USA, Commanding General, U.S. Third Army. Bradley and Patton were not actually involved in the southern France invasion. They were in northern France at the time.

Now, I had a front seat for this episode--they got the biggest sailors that were on board this vessel, the tallest ones, put these fellows over with all of the Army brass piggyback. One of the first down there was General Bradley. He comes down; and he had maps; he had binoculars; he had a tremendous amount of gear that he was bringing aboard the beach from the ship on this simulated assault.

But, either by malicious contriving or maybe he did lose his balance, that sailor lost his footing in the deepest water, and down he went. There was a bubbling of air bubbles and stuff; away floated the map of this, that, and the other thing; General Bradley came up and made it to the beach on his own power. This happened to every one of those sailors; they dumped their military load in the deep water. The fellows on board had to turn away to keep from laughing out loud, and some of them just couldn't help it. You could hear the laughter on board the LCI; this thing belonged in a Hal Roach comedy, not in a real-life thing. But that's what happened.

We do get that kind of comedy going on once in a while, just as happened aboard that transport carrying troops in for an assault. In the hold were the bedroom quarters--if we can use that term--for the GIs there. They were stacked in; maybe the ceiling would be 25 or 30 feet high, and they were given maybe 17 inches of space between bunks lined up there like in a shoe store in the old days, where you had a stepladder for the salesman to get up. But at each level there is another bunk space for some poor GI to get himself out flat and crawl in there, and that's where he did his night's rest. Somebody, going in for the assault, made the loud remark, "Is this trip necessary?" These are the things where American humor comes out, just as it did there on the beach at Salerno.

Q: Essential to break the tension too.

Commander Murray: But this is a long way around to get to the counterpart of the Halsey business with Admiral Kinkaid.

I had the same problem with Admiral Kinkaid when I was doing his portrait. The fighting had stopped, and Admiral Kinkaid was then Commander of the Eastern Sea Frontier, based down at 90 Church Street in New York.

Q: That was his last assignment, wasn't it, on active duty?

Commander Murray: I believe it was. He was a four-star admiral at the time and very senior. I had to find a

A. K. Murray #1 - 24

decent place to do this painting in. I couldn't find anyplace down at 90 Church Street, and then I discovered that J. P. Morgan's son Junius was a reserve captain in the Navy and his wife, I knew, was a Sunday painter.* They lived in a marvelous brownstone on 37th Street, right across the street from the Morgan Library. So I went up there and asked if he would importune on his good wife's nature to let us paint the admiral's portrait up there. He was delighted. So now we are up there doing this painting, and incidentally we painted Admiral Turner up there and several others.**

During this time, I couldn't get Admiral Kinkaid sobered up in the way that was needed, again to meet my requirements in painting at this time when the nation's honor is hanging by a thread, and the fortunes of war too are in a precarious position. I tried one episode after another. He, too, had been unhappy about Fletcher Pratt and some articles, and I was reluctant to get onto this Leyte Gulf thing, because I knew it bothered him deeply, having read The Saturday Evening Post two stories--Halsey versus Kinkaid version of it. But I finally did, and I really touched a nerve center.

Q: You got through that charm he possessed in retirement.

---
*John Pierpont Morgan was one of the country's best-known financiers in the early part of the 20th century.
**Admiral Richmond Kelly Turner, USN, whose portrait is discussed later in this oral history.

Admiral Thomas C. Kinkaid

Commander Murray: You see as commander of the Eastern Sea Frontier, the war was over, but he was still required to be in uniform, as I was and the rest of us. But he was wined and dined by all the hostesses on Park Avenue, and he was a great lion and he was in a happy mood--the wrong attitude altogether for me.

Q: Not a warrior, a perfectly charming man.

Commander Murray: Exactly. That is why I was so concerned to get back to the ugly side of some of the things he had to deal with. This man had spent over 40 years in the Navy, and now the great crisis had arrived. Now we are back to the Leyte Gulf campaign, because I knew that had deeply upset him. He was the first one that I brought this up to; I was doing his before I did Halsey's. This comment should have preceded comments on Halsey in these remarks.

Kinkaid was quartered in the marvelous Bullfinch House down in the Brooklyn Navy Yard at the time. He kindly invited me to have lunch with him each day down there. We would paint all day down there at Morgan studio. So when it came lunchtime we would jump in his car and go down there and have lunch and come back and work in the afternoon.

A. K. Murray #1 - 26

Since we were getting nowhere in the morning, I started this story around 11:00, having gotten nowhere on other issues before that. I didn't realize how deeply concerned he was with this issue. He started in, and the more he got talking about this thing, the more agitated he became. He got tremendously worked up, so it was getting just about to 12:00 o'clock and they liked an early lunch down there, so I adjourned our session and said, "Could we go now for lunch?"

"Good idea." So he lectured me all the way down to the navy yard about his side of the story. Then he disappeared as soon as we got in the front door; Mrs. Kinkaid came in and we sat down for a few minutes, and pretty soon the mess steward came in and said, "Lunch is ready, Mrs. Kinkaid, but the admiral is upstairs in his bedroom, and he won't come down. I knocked on his door."

She excused herself and went upstairs, and pretty soon she came down and said, "Tommy's a bit upset. He won't have lunch with us, but he'll go back with you when you go."

Q: You had gone a little too far.

Commander Murray: She was very discreet and didn't ask me what had been going on or anything, but I asked her was he all right, and she said, "Yes, he is all right; he is just upset. I think he'll eat a little something, and I have sent a tray up there." But as soon as I was through, I wanted to see what he was like and to get a better hold on this, because I was getting a bit concerned about this. And, as I say, he was a very senior officer. So we went back, and he lectured me all the way back, and after we got back into the studio--he was an inveterate smoker. He was somewhat of a chain smoker anyway, and his fingers were always brown with nicotine.

He would hardly light a cigarette before he had thrown that one away and got another, he was so nervous and agitated. The room was now full of smoke. I was concerned that he might have a heart attack or something. We had a good medical department right down there at 90 Church Street at that time, the headquarters for the Third Naval District, and I knew that could take good care of him. So I adjourned the session right then; we had hardly gotten started in the afternoon. About 45 minutes later, the butler came up from the household and said, "It's the Navy; they want to talk to you."

It turned out to be Lyons's aide, and he said, "What in God's name has been happening up there."

And I said, "What's the matter?", knowing darn well what probably was the matter.

And he said, "It's the admiral; he is terribly upset." He said, "He won't see anybody; he won't answer the telephone; the door is shut, and every time I go in there I can't see my way around, it's so dark even with the lights on. It's just filled with smoke; every ashtray is overloaded with cigarettes; he is pacing up and down on the floor, and I'm about to get the medical officer to come in and look him over."

I said, "I think that's a darn good idea," and then I told him what had happened.

"Oh my God, you really put your finger on a nerve center there." This had been going on since early morning, just working up to a horrible climax, and I could see him succumbing or some other ghastly episode.

It deeply impressed me afterward, the difference between the two men--Halsey and Kinkaid. Halsey was so phlegmatic, not at all of the temperament that Kinkaid was. The professional rivalry and jealousy, if you want to call it that, or whatever; there was a very sharp division. The mistake of one versus the non-mistake of the other made quite an impression on me. I had always made reservations about various officers in their capacity in these things, and I always had the feel that Admiral Halsey was a great fellow to tell his adversary, "Well, I'll meet you at latitude so-and-so, and longitude something-or-other, and we'll settle who is the top sea dog right then and there."

Whereas a fellow like this carrier force commander, Admiral Mitscher, would have a dozen battle plans in the

Vice Admiral Marc A. Mitscher

drawer of his desk there, and he would figure out if our first contacts indicate the enemy is such and such, this will be our procedure, and for so and so, we will try this; and for something or other, we'll try this and that. So he had done everything he can think of to meet the situation. With Halsey it was more of a slugfest or something else, with totally a different kind of temperament and personality.

There is another little episode to throw in at this point. Sometime later, I happened to have the radio on when I heard Admiral Halsey sounding off (there being no TV in those days) to the effect that he was going to ride the Japanese Emperor's white horse down the streets of Tokyo himself.* He was referring to the Japanese as those "dirty little yellow sons-of-bitches" and with just those words the radio was shut off.

Q: Censored.

Commander Murray: A few days later, he was back on the air. He was such a colorful fellow anyway, and he was warming up again to the subject and he said, "Those dirty, little, yellow--I'm not allowed to say it, but that's what they are just the same. The Secretary called me in a few days ago. I didn't abbreviate things like I am obliged to

---
*Actually, Halsey had made this pronouncement while the war was still in progress.

do it today, and I was instructed never to use those terms again, so I am complying with my instructions, hence the more reserved procedure today."

One more anecdote about Halsey, he had such a publicized face, sort of an old-man-of-the-mountain New Hampshire granite face that was well publicized with those bushy eyebrows and that craggy granite jaw of his and so on. The play Mr. Roberts had been well under way on Broadway, but the admiral had never been able to get in; he had made four tries, and every time he would go (this was at the time too when all the military still had to be in uniform). However, Henry Fonda had gotten out, and he was now having a lead role in this play. He had been in the Pacific Fleet during the war and knew the admiral rather well.*

So this was the fourth time Halsey had been turned around; the girl at the wicket never even looked up to see who was asking for a ticket. Even if she did, maybe she wouldn't recognize who it was even, although she should have. The admiral was alone, and when he was told there were no seats he was disconsolate and disgusted. As he got out on the sidewalk, Fonda was having a fast turn on a cigarette there, and he saw this familiar silhouette up the

---
*Mister Roberts was a stage adaptation of Thomas Heggen's comic novel about life on board a World War II cargo ship. See "Henry Fonda and the U.S. Navy," Naval History, Spring 1991, pages 77-79.

street, so he quickly rushed up and he said, "Oh, it is you, isn't it, Admiral. Were you trying to get in here by any chance?"

And he said, "Yes, I was and you can take your show and you know what you can do with it. This is the fourth time I can't get into the goddamn thing and blah, blah, blah."

"Now just calm down; we've got a seat for you. If we've got one for anybody, we've got one for you. Come along."

This is Admiral Halsey telling me about it, and he said, "To this day, I wouldn't have gotten in if I hadn't run into Fonda outside."

Q: How did Halsey impress you as a man in terms of intelligence? Was he an extremely intelligent man?

Commander Murray: I wouldn't put it that way; when you say extremely intelligent, I think of fellows like Raymond Spruance and Arleigh Burke and Tom Gates.* I don't put him in that class myself, but I don't presume to be any kind of a judge. I think Halsey was a great leader in the sense of having a certain charisma about him, but as far as

---

*Admiral Raymond A. Spruance, USN, Commander Fifth Fleet during World War II; Admiral Arleigh A. Burke, USN, Chief of Naval Operations from 1955 to 1961; Thomas S. Gates, Jr., Secretary of the Navy and Secretary of Defense during the Eisenhower Administration.

being brilliant or astute or shrewd, those are the characteristics that I don't feel readily attributable to him. I would to Marc Mitscher.

I think Mitscher was an extremely uncanny and shrewd kind of fellow who, by that thought "he who fights and runs away, lives to fight another day." He would back and fill and feint and be a terrific adversary. If he was confronted with inferior kind of equipment to face a superior thing, he would probably do a lot of pretty fast footwork that might save the day. Whereas I have the feeling Halsey would be more ponderous. He would be caught off base and he wouldn't have been able to collect himself in a crisis quite as fast as a fellow like Mitscher might have.

Q: Then you can apply that attribute to the San Bernardino Strait episode.

Commander Murray: I think so, especially with other officers present at the time who could evaluate what had been happening to the Japanese air arm, to come to a fair idea. However, here is another little digression at this point: I think that the flyboys (and I do not use it as a derogatory term) in this case the Army, I think in the European theater they had grossly overrated their bombing skills in Germany in which Speer pointed out, from the ground view of the Germans after these many industrial assaults, they would be back in business in the matter of a day or so.* From the reports of the Army Air Forces they were practically in rubble and ruin, and they wouldn't be productive for umpteen times again.

Q: The strategic bombing survey discovered that fact.

Commander Murray: Yes, that is what I am trying to point out about this type of attitude. The same, I think, often in evaluating the Pacific side of the war--in my opinion, the weapon that brought Japan to its knees was not the airplane; it was the submarine. And because the submarine destroyed Japan's capacity to support their far-flung bases, and without these bases the war would grind to a halt. The air assaults on the mainland, in my opinion, weren't the coup de grace that brought Japan down; it was the submarine.

Q: You finally completed the painting of Halsey?

Commander Murray: Yes, I had him aboard what would appear to be a carrier of the Enterprise class with aircraft in the background with a heavy somber sky and a threatening sea to rather simulate the whole business, mindful of the

---
*Albert Speer was Germany's Minister of Armaments during World War II.

A. K. Murray #1 - 34

uncertain forces of war and the fact that we, at one point, had practically nothing. And then back in the beginning in the Guadalcanal business when we had to use Catalina aircraft as dive bombers, an aircraft that makes probably 150 knots. We just had nothing, and the only carriers we had were the old-timers like the _Saratoga_. Then at the close of the war we had 105 of them. On one of these marvelous Steichen photos they were lined up there, at Ulithi; they went clear over the horizon.*

The 105 carriers were an incredible kind of an armada that had never existed in the world before. So in these paintings during the war, I was trying to be mindful of some of the significant problems that we had overcome or were trying to overcome, that made the achievements all that more credible. Like, for instance, in this Halsey portrait there is no sunny skies, no bravado; the thing is very touchy.

Q: And you did achieve that warrior-like attitude in Halsey.

Commander Murray: I feel that we had an aggressive thing where the handle Bull Halsey would apply. This is a man of

---

*Edward Steichen, one of the pioneers in the use of photography as an art form, was commissioned as a Naval Reserve officer during World War II and headed a combat camera team which turned out some remarkable work.

resolute resolve, iron stamina, and chrome steel will, and as long as he's got a leg to stand on he is going to swing a hefty punch if he can. And he'll go down swinging if he has to go down, and you will know you have really tangled with an adversary, but he might not have to go down if he had a little more agility on some of the other things, like some of these other officers. That is only a personal opinion, and I don't mean it in a negative way; there is room for both people. I think Halsey was a great catalyst in the public relations way of getting an esprit de corps and in the rallying of the public and the nation and all that.

Q: He certainly was wonderful at that point in stimulating the populace of the country. Did you also succeed in somehow or other depicting this charismatic characteristic of his, or was that not possible in the overriding sense?

Commander Murray: I would perhaps say that he could be understood as an attractive man in that sense, as a magnetic sort of fellow. He isn't somebody you would pass by quickly or, shall we say, a nonentity. His very appearance was something to encourage a second look. Even in passing him on the street, if you are sensitive to people's appearances, his was an appearance that would make an impression on you. As to the word charismatic, I would

A. K. Murray #1 - 36

say yes, I think he had charisma, but whether I was able to convey it, I would have to ask somebody else. I was aware of this thing and was hoping to do it, but whether I succeeded or not is hardly for me to say. I hope I did. I was aware of it and tried to.

Q: What was the reaction of the two Halseys to the portrait when it was completed?

Commander Murray: I think they were quite happy with it. I don't recall negative responses by anybody to it. Sometimes people are that way.

I have had, if you will recall, with Bud Zumwalt's portrait, both he and his wife and his aide thought I made him look sad in it, and my response was that I did it deliberately.* I thought that was part of my problem, and I would do it again if I was to start over again. I don't look upon these things, I am not trying to please the individual; I am approaching this thing as a piece of documentation, as a significant portrait of a man in a certain role and a dedicated life. Getting back to that aspect--this is a revealing business on Al Murray as well as it is on these people he is talking about.

Q: Yes, indeed it is. A very broad-gauged Al Murray, I might add.

---
*Admiral Elmo R. Zumwalt, Jr., USN, Chief of Naval Operations from 1970 to 1974.

Admiral Elmo R. Zumwalt

Commander Murray: After all, this is the life I have chosen to live, and I have tried to be as effective as I am capable of doing, and so I am always hypercritical trying to find out what my weak spots are and bolster them up, hone the good ones and get as sharp an edge as I can. In the case of Admiral Zumwalt why I had him looking sad--this is a subtle thing. People would only see this after prolonged observation if they are highly sensitive to him.

The reason for my doing it was that he was not like Admiral Kinkaid at the time. The pressure of the war was over, and we were now facing, presumably, a long peacetime tour, and a man running a top military command in peacetime is in a far different pressure cooker than somebody who is running the outfit at a time of war when there is open season on him, in all directions, by everybody--the Congress, the administration in the White House, the whole military household, the public. He is on the spot for potshots from all directions by everybody, especially if things are not going well. Whether he is to blame or personally involved very often is beside the point; simply being in uniform brands him as being part and parcel of the whole package.

Back to Zumwalt, the thing is that we were in the most unpopular war in our history, the Vietnamese thing. That's an up and down kind of a thing and for the most part was progressing on the downside. The public was extremely unhappy with it. There is another major episode that was occurring for the incumbent of the command that was running the Navy. We had a major social upheaval in our whole social structure in the nation. Long hair, disheveled appearance, unshaven, for the men their shirttails are put in, they don't shave. The whole attitude of the male populace in the nation has taken a gigantic change, in my own opinion, for the downgrade side of things. Now some of these candidates were appearing in the Navy. You've got this great upheaval on the campuses where the ROTC--you hear whispers that research buildings and laboratories that are involved in military contracts are being burned down; the flag is being burned. We are in terrible shape socially.

Now, some of these same people are at sea in the Navy, or in the Marine Corps, in spite of sorting and sifting and doing whatever you can as you recruit them. You get, sifting through a lot of unfortunate people on board ship to where you got a sitdown strike aboard the Constellation, an unheard of kind of a thing.* You've got over 60 or more people who refuse to do their job, so what are you going to do, prefer a general court-martial? The ship was practically immobilized due to this sit-down strike, and

---

*For more on this episode, see Captain Paul B. Ryan, USN (Ret.), "USS Constellation Flare-up: Was it Mutiny?" U.S. Naval Institute Proceedings, January 1976, pages 46-53.

they are at sea; they are not tied up in a port; there is a war going on. This is an incredible kind of business. The admiral in command here is not somebody that has just left a Park Avenue hostess with cigars and brandy and everything is in mothballs insofar as the military is concerned.

It is a case of life and death, and people are dying right now and more will be dying tomorrow. We're going to lose some ships, and we're going to lose some more aircraft; this thing is a rough kind of business. I don't know whether the admiral had a son in the air arm; it seemed to me that he did and that he would have to volunteer too. All of these things would add up to a very deeply concerned aspect for the most part.

Q: A note of sadness.

Commander Murray: A deep-rooted and a thoroughly understandable one, as long as he is in this role and he loves the Navy and he is doing his level best. He's a highly trained and a highly intelligent individual; he feels he can make substantial contributions and he wants to, so he doesn't exercise the only other option he has, which is to get out. Either do what the administration directs as the Commander in Chief, or his only other option is to retire. But he is in, and he wants to do these things and he feels he can make these contributions, and

A. K. Murray #1 - 40

that explains this extremely sober, responsible look that I have tried to get in this portrait.

Q: That is a fascinating point to have made. Let me go back once more to Halsey and ask another question. Did the admiral eventually understand what you were driving at when you were trying to recreate things and make him angry and arouse his temper?

Commander Murray: I am sure he did.

Q: You never reached the point of discussing it afterward?

Commander Murray: No, he wasn't the kind of man that I could get into these things. He wasn't interested very much in this whole aspect of the thing. He had very little vanity; he didn't have an ego that was very much in the way. I wasn't aware of that. There have been other people--so many times a sitter--to use that term as a painter--expresses keen interest in the whole procedure of what your objectives are from session to session, and how they can contribute and the whole thing. Halsey wasn't disposed; this was just another job, another assignment, and he was dedicated to do what he was told to do in the sense of his military training. Whatever was required of him to do, he would do it and do it to the best of his ability. But discussing the pros and cons and the niceties about the painting was not of interest to him.

In great contrast to this was a recent painting of Bob Barrow for the Marine Corps.* He was extremely interested, and so was Jimmy Holloway.**

Q: I would expect that Holloway would.

Commander Murray: They wanted to know exactly what I was trying to do, and I enjoyed telling them, and then they would cooperate beautifully because they too could see before we got started: "Here is what I hope will happen before you leave today; we are trying to deal with this thing and we are trying to do this with it." I would often put up a cardboard between the source of light and the painting to show a change of value on it, where this is reduced in importance on the painting in order to get the observer's attention back up to the primary target, which would be the head, by killing other passages in the canvas. So the observer, without being aware of it, was being directed by the painter to see what he wanted them to see.

But at the same time when interest there had wandered and he was now exploring other areas of the canvas, he would come down to the hands or other aspects but then be

---
*General Robert H. Barrow, USMC, Commandant of the Marine Corps from 1979 to 1983.
**Admiral James L. Holloway III, USN, Chief of Naval Operations from 1974 to 1978.

Admiral James L. Holloway III

gently led back again to the primary target--just as the stage electrician illuminates the players on the stage so that the audience sees what the director wants them to see, when he wants them to see it. All the fill-in stuff is also around there and they are playing their part, but they are not upstaging the matinee idol with it; he has to show that that is where the thing is, due to the lighting and the arrangement.

The problems of how you do this from a painting standpoint would be of interest to them too, and that also helped me in getting their cooperation to come on back, because sometimes this stuff would be easily obtained, and sometimes it was incredibly full of attrition and a lot of blood, sweat, and tears would go into the thing until you could make it happen. And it's got to happen spontaneously without looking to be fought over and struggled for; that's got to be kept out of it, even though you were exhausted and quartered and drawn to get there. The observer must never be aware of that thing; it must look like it just happened. That takes a dual cooperation between the painter and the sitter. That is why I particularly am happy when I find people who respond to these problems and give you a good time instead of a bad time, to use a phrase that is often used today.

Q: You have to be then something of a Svengali as well as an artist, in manipulating people.

Commander Murray: These things help. It is a two-way street, but you need to try to make these things happen as best you can without asking. You can't say, "Well, now smile" or something like that. As I mentioned earlier, these things can often look contrived then and not spontaneous. It is when they happen; it is just like a sudden beam of sunlight that broke through the clouds; it is a wonderful kind of thing that just happens. If you force a thing and get it turned on, it is often not the same thing at all; it is tiresome; it is worked over; it has lost its punch.

Q: Let's go back for a moment to another loose end, and that is Admiral Kinkaid. When you really upset him far beyond what you had expected, were you able to catch this warrior attitude which you had hoped to achieve under those circumstances, or did you have to abandon it for the time being?

Commander Murray: He was a much more easily persuaded fellow to get into a sober attitude than Halsey. He was much easier to deal with than Halsey, in that respect.

A. K. Murray #1 - 44

Q: But you never could precipitate this sort of thing again?

Commander Murray: No, but I didn't need to. When we got into the room again and we got onto this subject, it was just as if he was automatically reminded of it for the balance of our sessions that we had.

Q: It almost disrupted your rapport with him then, did it?

Commander Murray: No, he would be in a pretty sober kind of mood. I don't know; children sometimes get that way if they are put back into the same atmosphere where some punishment occurred. It is sort of like what Jimmy Holloway said, "You know, being with you I feel sort of like I am with my shrink and I am on the psychiatrist's couch in here." That is an actual quote from what Jimmy had to say.

Q: There is a certain amount of that.

Commander Murray: That I think answers what I was trying to say about Admiral Kinkaid--that, for the remaining times when we were dealing with this confrontation, the two of us, he was more or less drawn back onto that issue, knowing that this was what I was trying at the time in his military

A. K. Murray #1 - 45

life, that I was trying to convey. Whether he wanted to or not, when we were face to face he was more than likely swinging into that rather than into whatever other episodes he had been tangled up with before we were face to face.

Q: So you really had achieved, on a permanent basis, what you had set out to do on that occasion?

Commander Murray: He would be cordial enough in a social way when we might encounter each other back in his quarters or something else on another issue but, in the studio, no.

Q: I don't think I have ever seen your portrait of Admiral Kinkaid, but I am aware of this--did you do the full-length one of Kinkaid and Mrs. Kinkaid that they had in their drawing room in Washington?

Commander Murray: No. The one of Admiral Kinkaid is represented in the admiral's quarters at sea, and I have a flag lieutenant coming through the hatch there with some sort of a dispatch. I used myself as the flag lieutenant there at that time. But as to identity, practically you couldn't recognize who it was. I wanted a dark, somber interior, and I now have forgotten the ship that I used. It is a very simple, dark interior, sort of a dark maroon wall that prevailed in that ship, and dark furniture, so the only object of illumination is the admiral himself. It is about only a three-quarter length. The one of Admiral Halsey--he is seated in that little chair welded onto the rail up on the bridge that an officer could sit in there; it is sort of like a boatswain's chair that is welded right onto the bulkhead there. That just ends below the knees. Both of them are just below the knees; they are not full-length paintings.

Q: We are now talking about the Zumwalt portrait again.

Commander Murray: You are asking about the Zumwalt one. I felt that I was more successful maybe in that one than many. I would like to say, however, in all humility that when you are in this thing as deeply as I am--I married a paint brush; my whole life is wrapped up in this darn thing, trying to paint portraits and trying to make them as good as I can. The humble truth of the matter is no matter how good you make it, it could probably be a darn sight better, so what you are always looking under the rug for and digging around for is trying to find out those things that would help you to reach a better plateau. No matter where it is, there is always some way that that could occur, and you are trying to find out what some of those might be. However, I think in general, the various ingredients that I was hoping to get in there, I had unusually good success with the Zumwalt one. That is a good composition; the color is good; the painterly aspects are all good ones.

Q: And a striking pose--that profile.

Commander Murray: That is part of the thing. You see, a painting becomes commonplace or distinguished in the mind of the painter before anything is applied to the canvas. It is how he sees and thinks about the thing as to whether it gets up off the ground and soars, or whether it is very earthbound and pedestrian.

Q: Similar to the sculptor, isn't it, who sees it in the marble before he ever begins to chisel?

Commander Murray: That is why it's difficult and takes a bit of time when somebody comes to the door for you to start this portrait. You can't just plunk them down in a chair, pick up your tools, and start to work. If you do that, you may discover during a rest period that a perfectly magnificent attitude has occurred. Now you throw away the first one and start that one. In your first proceeding with these things, you like to get the biography of the fellow ahead of time and think about what his life is about and what his role is and where this thing is supposed to go, what kind of an environment it will be in and what sort of an audience it will be facing mostly. All of these sort of ingredients can sort of bounce around in your consciousness, and then when he is here to try all sorts of attitudes. And then, a very significant thing is to have rest times when you are particularly sharp to see what he does. He may do something--he may light up a cigarette now, or sit down in utter exhaustion, or scratch himself or do something else that suggests something that is far better than anything else that has happened so far. So you're the hunter in a duck blind with both barrels loaded, sort of hiding in the bushes there ready to fire as soon as the target has done something that you can't miss. You are looking for all of these things without the subject being aware of it.

Q: Do you engage him in conversation during rest periods?

Commander Murray: Yes, sure.

Q: On just extraneous things, or what?

Commander Murray: Anything that might turn him on, or, if they are of a very reticent nature and so on, you might want to shut it all off to let him be quiet and see what happens. The role of the painter--his radar is turning

A. K. Murray #1 - 49

around full blast the whole time that he is in there, fully conscious of what may be taking place, hoping that something is going to happen, that he will have the good fortune to see it when it happens and to respond to it when it occurs. That is how these things can be distinguished or commonplace; often you happen to catch something that lifts it away from the day-to-day, something that establishes it.

Q: Al, if you would say something more about the Zumwalt portrait as such. A few years ago you told me the story of how you had to work to get the right angle for the jaw. I wonder if you would repeat that again, because if you got it at a different angle it showed him as a different kind of person.

Commander Murray: These things are all very pertinent--the matter of technique. This would probably be a discussion in a portrait painter's class, when you are trying to alert the students to some of the nuances that go on. In this case with Zumwalt, he had a very fine, aristocratic head; the whole skeleton was one perfectly beautiful, aristocratic aspect of the features. Also, I have spent some time in Portugal, and his complexion was a bit olive; he looked very much to me like a Portuguese aristocrat, very handsome and sort of a noble aspect. I took 180 degrees around with his head, looking at the various aspects and felt more keen about the profile, so now I eliminated all other aspects in my approach, so it was the head itself, not the torso. The head I would do with the profile.

Now, I was trying to find the torso that would best simulate a sense of confidence and robust vigor and so on, to support this head. To make this area interesting I used the cap and the hand with the gloves and settled on the torso, so now we've got the figure tied down from where the observer is going to see it. On deciding the tilt of the head on the up-and-down axis, whether to raise the chin or lower it, or to gaze--and where the eyes are to look has a good deal to do with this too for the psychological effect, so that the sensitive observer will read into it appropriate things and not the wrong things. I decided the exact tilt of his head would be very significant, because if I tilted it down he could look indecisive or unsure of what he often wanted to do. If I tilted it up beyond where I have it, it could have an aspect of arrogance--"Do it my way and never mind anything else"--a closed-mind attitude, and I didn't want that.

I wanted a thoughtful, considered attitude about questions of importance where all sides would be heard and listened to whether he liked them or not, and possibly something useful was of value here and he didn't want to miss it. So I didn't want this arrogant look; neither did I want the indecisive connotation in a lowered position from where I have it. I am speaking now of an up-and-down basis, staying on the same target that I have on the profile, and that motivated the precise position where it is now. It is a forthright, candid one, which is neither indecisive nor arrogant. So that I zeroed in on the best of the three choices there, which had to do with why the head is exactly where it is on this thing.

This is not accident in any kind of way. No part of this whole darn rectangle, the painting and the concept, not by accident. It is all by careful consideration of this kind of thing, and you don't get that way overnight. My own judgments I sometimes want to verify substantially, so if I am in a very touchy area I would like to leave it that way overnight and not go any further with it, just to eliminate further problems in getting it off the canvas if I thought I needed to adjust it. So when I think I am satisfied and have got the right theme in, I would generally leave it and come at it cold the next day to see if I am still in agreement.

Sometimes I am not, and I would never hesitate to make drastic changes if I feel that I am in error, as I can sometimes be. Usually the first impulses are generally apt to be the more reliable ones. That is not always so, and I always like to be reassured about these things. So I would turn it to the wall, and in the final analysis too on that same subject I often turn the thing to the wall when I tell the sitter we are finished and then get it out of my system with succeeding paintings. And when I think I have pretty well gotten it out of my system, I'll turn it around and take a good look at it again and see if I am still comfortable about it. If I am, it's ready to be sent out; if not, we're going to be back into it again. That way I feel I am trying to wring myself out to get the best that I am able to put into it.

A lot of times significant things can happen, just as leaving it in the studio where it can be seen every time I walk by, or cut the light off, or put on artificial light at night I sort of subconsciously consider it when I go by it or see it. Certain things can happen, as another shadow that appeared on it, or something else has happened to give me new thoughts that might be an improvement for it. I am sort of constantly with these things.

It is not like, a sitter once said to me, doing an outdoor scene, a shooting scene in his very expensive shooting jacket and a horribly expensive shotgun and all that. He said, "For God's sake why don't you just paint a sky and be done with it?" Well, that is the opposite of the good type of sitter. The man had no consideration whatever of what goes into the sky, because the problem was to support everything else. It's like a beautiful stone for a jeweler who is going to make a ring out of it. The setting has to be something that compliments the stone and distinguished from the merits of the stone, but it must not be competitive with it, saying, "Look at me instead of look at the stone." It's got to be there and not be there, but it has got to also be of great distinction and ability of an appropriate nature.

The same with the sky; when you break it down into the skeleton of its pattern, it must support and repeat and echo aspects that prevail in the figure itself, so that it's a first cousin to the figure, and they are intimately related, and you can't rearrange and adjust without a sacrificial cost. The thing ought to be that right when you finally leave it, that further tinkering with it is going to be negative instead of productive. At that point, you leave it alone, and you probably have it by then. These are the things that make it somewhat tedious for some sitters, when they think, "Why in the world aren't you through with the darn thing?" You just want to make sure that you have gone about as far as you can with it.

Q: In the case of the Zumwalt portrait, was the admiral aware of your objectives and did he discuss them with you?

A. K. Murray #1 - 54

Did he cooperate? Was he interested?

Commander Murray: I, of course, never got onto the subject the way I have with you. It would be disastrous, I think, for me to talk as candid with him as I have with you, because he would be so self-conscious and embarrassed about it. He is a modest fellow, and I hold Zumwalt in very high regard in many respects, although I am fully aware that many of his colleagues are distinctly unhappy with him. I think certain things occurred during his tour of duty that I think have boomeranged for him in an unfortunate way which he is not at all deserving.

I think we are indebted to him for surveying a lot of ships and getting a lot of new construction going on, which a less perceptive kind of fellow might not have done. And we could be hurting still more today if we didn't have a Zumwalt perception on some of these issues which he brought about and which we are the better for them today than we would have been without them. He is a dedicated kind of man; he is a great patriot, although others criticize him, wanting to make extremely unfortunate observations, which I think are grossly undeserved.

I think anybody who is aggressive in a role like his is bound to be controversial, and some of this controversy I think is grossly unfounded. As I say, this is a personal reaction. I wouldn't have discussed some of these personal

A. K. Murray #1 - 55

issues with him, simply because it would have defeated my purpose. He would have become so uncomfortable and ill at ease that I would have defeated myself.

Q: But in the case of some of the other men you were able to do this?

Commander Murray: I am aware of a kind of barrier there, and we didn't have that barrier with the others. In fact, it was helpful to talk with them about it, I got more out of them. We were old cronies with the same mutual target that we were shooting for; it was a very different kind of a ball game. This other aspect was something else again; it was sort of like asking somebody to smile or not to smile.

Q: In the case of the Zumwalt portrait, which I think is the best one I have seen of yours, I was terribly enthusiastic about it when I took it down to Washington and to Annapolis. But in the case of that, did it please him? Did he understand afterward, for instance, the angle of the jaw and that sort of thing?

Commander Murray: I don't know whether he did or not. I sometimes like, when we are all through, to explain some of these things to the layman, because naturally they would not be expected to guess these things unless they are more or less a student of these things.

Q: To begin to understand that complexity of the task?

Commander Murray: Yes, and he was very cooperative to me so that I didn't have to feel the need to go into this in extra innings. I do this deliberately sometimes in order to get them to play ball with me because--this seems to be a most stupid remark to make having spent nearly 50 years in this business. To be perfectly honest, I don't know how long a thing is going to take me when we start in, and I have been doing these things day after day after day my entire life. The darnedest things get in the way to drag it out or to shorten it. It could make a rough average, but we can be way over it or once in a while we are under it.

Q: There are so many intangibles involved in the task.

Commander Murray: Well, there are, but so many times the sitter expects this to be a rather quick kind of procedure.

Q: I suppose the man with the gun and the hunting jacket was that kind.

Commander Murray: He wasn't alone.

Q: He was a business type, I assume.

Commander Murray: Yes, but here in the military, too, most people have no conception really about what is involved from a painter's point of view, none whatever. I like to feel that I can get all the cooperation that I need from the sitter and to be met halfway down this two-way street and not have to fight for the time that I need to make the journey that I feel I am capable of making. So many times I don't get that; it is standard not to get it.

Now, when I was doing General Chapman, for instance, of the Marine Corps, he grasped right away what my problems were, and I explained some of them to him.* When I did, I couldn't get more cooperation. He was leaning over backward; he said, "How many more times you want me to come, just tell me. I'll be here." It was just what I could dream of to help me go where I felt capable of going, as against having to cajole and fight and beg and bribe and everything else like you would for a child, whom you can understand just hates the whole process and would do anything to escape it. You don't expect that from a disciplined adult. They ought to be able to make themselves do what is unpleasant and uncomfortable.

---
*General Leonard F. Chapman, Jr., USMC, Commandant of the Marine Corps from 1968 to 1971.

General Leonard F. Chapman

Q: When you run into that, I suppose you have to play on a man's vanity or what-have-you in order to achieve it.

Commander Murray: You do anything you can to get it. To get these moods, to create the circumstances in which the mood will take place spontaneously is another big chore, and that is wholly apart from your training in art school to draw what you are looking at. If it is still life, it is going to be there day after day, but when you are dealing with a human expression, it may only be there once in days and not very long. So you need to recognize it when you see it and then try to create the circumstances in which it is apt to reoccur so you can get a second and a third and a fourth look at it in trying to tie it down.

Q: In the case of the Zumwalt portrait, as a matter for the record, how many times did you see him? How many times did he sit for you?

Commander Murray: I would have to look at my diary in order to tell, but whatever they were he supplied willingly, not grudgingly and Jimmy Holloway the same, also Bob Barrow.

Q: Once you got him under way, but he did not at first?

Commander Murray: It was tough going to start with, and I think he chafed under that and then resolved to be as cooperative as he could. No one could be any more cooperative than Zumwalt was when we got started. Any of these, once they understand what it is all about--and I hate tyranny anyway of the artist in ordering people around. There is classic example here of Whistler doing a portrait of an Englishwoman of the peerage.* Her father was the butcher to the king and was finally knighted, so Whistler is now doing this woman's portrait. And he tells her in an adamant fashion, "You be at the studio on Wednesday at 10:00 o'clock." Now, she is supposed to shove off and reappear at 10:00, and she got fed up with this tyranny so on one of those Wednesdays at 10:00 o'clock she sent her maid with her ermine and the whole getup. Whistler was so incensed that he rubbed out her face and he painted the maid's picture.

Q: Now we are going to turn our attention to Admiral Thomas Hart.**

---

*James Abbott McNeill Whistler (1834-1903) was a noted American painter and etcher. He did much of his work in London and Paris.
**Admiral Thomas C. Hart, USN, who was Commander in Chief of the U.S. Asiatic Fleet from 1939 until the fleet went out of existence in early 1942. He was on the General Board of the Navy from 1942 to 1945.

Admiral Thomas C. Hart

Commander Murray: There are two thoughts about him--one at the time of the painting and then some nearly 30 years later.

Q: That is one of your most beautiful portraits.

Commander Murray: I like that aspect, the white uniform and the pince-nez glasses and the cigarette and the whole thing. Admiral Hart was the next to the last to come to the General Board. That was a World War II outfit to create jobs for very senior admirals.

Q: Wasn't this when he returned from the Far East?

Commander Murray: Yes, that was where he wound up, and he was the senior officer in the General Board.

Q: And chairman, I think.

Commander Murray: Yes, he was, at the time I was doing this. My first portrait assignment in this Combat Art Section was to paint portraits of the General Board. I thought that Admiral Hart would be best in a white uniform. He was sort of giving me a hard time about this whole thing; he didn't warm up to it worth a darn in any respect.

Q: You mean he didn't want his portrait painted?

Commander Murray: Something to that effect. I painted his predecessor in the Far East command, Harry Yarnell.* He was the first admiral that I had ever painted as an artist. Admiral Yarnell preceded Hart in the Augusta out there, and Admiral Hart brought the Augusta back. I had done Admiral Yarnell in whites, full length. It is now in the Naval Academy; I gave it to the Naval Academy as a present later on. Admiral Yarnell and I became extremely close friends. He became a godfather to me, and it was due to him that I came into the Navy in the first place, as against the Army. I had a commission in the cavalry--they were horse cavalry in the Army at the time--but through various circumstances and one thing or another, it managed to get switched around and they weren't going to activate a bunch of us in the reserve and the national guard in the cavalry for month after month after month. And Pearl Harbor had finished and I wanted to get active, so I managed to get into the Navy via help from Admiral Yarnell.

I persuaded Admiral Hart finally. He claimed he didn't have any white uniform. I said, "Well, you're about the same size; would you wear mine?" I don't know whether he really didn't have any or what; anyway, he is wearing my

---
*Admiral Harry E. Yarnell, USN, was Commander in Chief of the Asiatic Fleet from 1936 to 1939.

Admiral Harry E. Yarnell

A. K. Murray #1 - 62

uniform in that portrait, with his shoulder boards, of course.

Q: Where did you paint him? In Washington?

Commander Murray: Yes, in the Corcoran Gallery. The Corcoran was very kind to make that--they had at the time (but no longer, it is something else now) a perfectly marvelous studio. I painted a great many portraits in there, including Admiral Nimitz and Admiral Leahy.* It is a superb studio.

Q: I knew that studio--beautiful light there.

Commander Murray: Excellent light and a good sized place. I did James Forrestal's portrait in there and a whole batch of them.**

So we finally got started with this, and the admiral and I seemed to warm up very well in a sitter-artist relationship. I had gotten filled in about many of the admiral's responses to others in the Navy when he was known as "high-collar Hart" and when he was superintendent and he ran a very taut ship.*** And then he very kindly, in

---
*Fleet Admiral William D. Leahy, USN, chief of staff to the Commander in Chief during and after World War II.
**James V. Forrestal, Secretary of the Navy during the latter part of World War II and then first Secretary of Defense after the services were unified.
***Admiral Hart had been Superintendent of the Naval Academy from 1931 to 1934.

warming up here, had me out to his house, and we got on to a very happy relationship.

Q: I trust you discovered his wonderful sense of humor?

Commander Murray: Yes, and I got to meet his family and his daughter and so on, in the apartment he had out on Connecticut Avenue. I remember a very embarrassing episode in which he had asked me if I had ever had a gimlet, and I said, "No, I haven't."

And he said, "That's a drink we have a lot in the Far East," and he said, "What are you doing tonight? Come on out to dinner if you can."

So out there in his apartment he had a jar full of these gimlets and he said, "Here, let's try one of these," so his daughter Isabella was there at the time and she, perfectly charming, brought these things in and so we had one and he said, "You liked it didn't you?"

I said, "Sure, it tasted just like fruit juice, what else is in it?"

And he said, "It's mostly fruit juice and gin." I'm not much of a drinking man; we had two of those. He didn't tell me that anybody else was coming and then he announced, "My old classmate, Harry Yarnell, is coming to dinner." By this time, as I say, Admiral Yarnell and I were extremely close. I looked upon him as a godfather. Suddenly the doorbell rang, and the admiral jumped up and said, "I think that's Harry now." We are all in uniform and I attempted to get up and to my horror--my mind was clear as a bell, but my knees were made out of rubber; I had to hold onto a chair. It was the most embarrassing situation I can recall getting into. It was those darned drinks that we were having.

Q: That was an unfair advantage.

Commander Murray: I heard him say to Admiral Yarnell, "Our friend Al Murray is in here. He is going to have dinner with us, and I have to tell you ahead of time, he has never had a gimlet before and I have given him a couple and I am not quite sure he is very comfortable with them, so we may have to carry him into the dining room." When I heard that, it was all the more embarrassing to me, but I was out of the chair, on my feet but holding onto the chair when he came in. Then, when Isabella announced dinner, the two of them did literally each take one side of me, like policemen with a culprit in between to take him to the paddy wagon, as we go into the dining room. This was the most awkward thing, with a crystal clear head and nothing wrong except that my propulsion gear was out of whack. But it soon straightened out. I confided all this to the admiral later on, by which he was highly amused. But I thought that was dirty politics to do that to me.

A later incumbent, the last one to come into the General Board that I was familiar with was Admiral Kalbfus.* I will get back to Hart in a minute, because this has a great deal to do with Kalbfus. Kalbfus I had known in Newport where I had been doing a lot of painting before I came into the Navy. That is where I did Admiral Yarnell's full-length portrait. If I as a painter was going down the sidewalk looking for a model and Kalbfus appeared, I would rush over to him and beg him to come into the studio.

As a real salty sea dog, Kalbfus looked the part. He had a rolling gait and he had no neck. His bullet head sat right on his shoulders, and he had an enormous torso. His upper arm was like the thigh of most men; it was enormous. He had a bald head that shone like the simonized fender of a freshly simonized automobile. He had enormous girth, a terrific avoirdupois. So when he showed up for his portrait, I was a senior lieutenant. I think that's what I was. At any rate, I was pretty low down on the totem pole.

He was thinking of me now as this civilian he used to know in Newport. So he tells me just how I am supposed to

---

*Rear Admiral Edward C. Kalbfus, USN (Ret.) had served a four-star tour as Commander Battle Force in 1938-1939. As a rear Admiral, he served as president of the Naval War College from 1934 to 1936 and from June 1939 to June 1942. As a four-star admiral on the retired list, he was president of the War College from June to November 1942.

do this. He said, "I want to be covered." (He didn't like his bald head.) And he said, "You know, I have lost a lot of weight since your Newport days, and I want that to appear." Well, I just couldn't miss the chance that the man afforded. He was terrific, so I had him uncovered, seated at a table with one elbow up on it where you had this great big forearm and then all the gold braid up there--high rank--and this enormous tummy had to be accommodated by keeping his knees apart because of the bulbous girth. He had to have his legs apart, and then the buttons on his blue uniform were like marks on a contour map, a geology study of the various contour marks.

When he took a look at that, he said, "My God, you have done everything I told you not to." So he wouldn't speak to me then, but he used to come back for each sitting, but he would never speak to me. By this time, Admiral Hart wanted to know how it was getting on, so he would be in telephone contact with me every day, and I would tell him. These were daily sessions, and I would tell him blow by blow, troubles I was having. He said, "Now just keep your shirt on, Al. Don't worry; we'll take care of Dutch. Don't be upset about it."

When I got through, I told the admiral, "Would you like to have Mrs. Kalbfus come over?"* I knew her quite well too from Newport days.

---
*Syria Brown Kalbfus

Rear Admiral Edward C. Kalbfus

So he said, "Yes, but she has had a small accident; she is in a wheelchair. If you don't mind, we'll bring her up in the wheelchair."

I said, "Fine, there is a back courtyard here, and we use the freight elevator right here, and I'll meet you downstairs with the wheelchair." So at the appropriate time I am down there with the wheelchair, and in he comes. He carried her out of the sedan, and placed her in the wheelchair. She had always fancied herself as a frustrated thespian, a Sarah Bernhardt or something. She always had a big picture hat on her head and a lorgnette. When he was running the Naval War College is when I knew them in Newport, and I had seen them very often at many social functions in Newport. One time she had invited me to come to the war college for a Sunday affair that they were having. This is during the early part of the war, we weren't in it yet; this is when all the 50 destroyers were still up there in Newport before they got turned over.

Brenda Harvey was there; she was of the family that made the Harvey's Bristol Cream, an English girl who was very buxom and a very attractive creature and a good friend of mine. She was invited to this party too. It was a standard Sunday affair for the president of the war college. Mrs. Kalbfus didn't call me by name at this other dinner party. When she invited me, she said, "Mr. Uh, Mr.

A. K. Murray #1 - 68

Thingamajig, I'd like you to come to our open house on Sunday."

That upset me so, knowing darn well what my name was. I looked at her and said, "Mrs. uh, Mrs. Whatdoyoucallit, I'll be delighted." Her eyes nearly popped out of her head.

Q: She dropped her lorgnette?

Commander Murray: Yes, she didn't say anything, but she got the message. So now we are at the party. As you may recall, at the war college there is this front door where most everybody comes and then there is a side entrance. There was a Marine sentry at each entrance, and I came through the side entrance. Brenda was standing by the table where the canapes and the principal bar was, and the admiral was right across there. Brenda had this very low-cut gown on, and she was leaning over to pick up something from the table and I couldn't resist the temptation. I pulled a quarter out of my pocket, tossed it over, and made a basket; it went right down her bosom. She always enjoyed the light touch, so she did a little shimmy dance. The quarter rolled on the floor and rolled right back toward me.

The sentry saw the whole business, and the admiral saw the whole business. He saw me toss it and everything, and he saw the quarter roll back. He saw the sentry pick it up and hand it to me. Well, I thought Kalbfus was going to blow a fuse then, but he didn't say anything, and Brenda just gave me a sort of look--"Not bad, we both did pretty well, didn't we?"--kind of look on her face, and that was all there was to that. He was pretty frosty then.

So with this little episode we move back to when I am doing his portrait, and I am not doing what he wanted. So he didn't speak to me. Now he brought Mrs. Kalbfus in; she was witness to this little episode at the war college too. When I met her down at the door with the car and he put her in the wheelchair, the elevator was slightly out of phase and you couldn't make a precise landing, so I had to lift the front wheels up to the inch difference or whatever on the level, then lift the rear wheels and get her up. I did it as gently as a baby, but she acted as though the thing had been bounced over a pothole and winced terribly, as though you had a commando's bayonet up her back or something, and the admiral looked at me as much as to say, "Look, don't be upset with this; you don't live with it. I live with it."

The same thing happened when we got to the stop level. You just pushed this button and the same out of phase, and we had a repeat of the episode getting her off on that level, again with this awful wincing agony. It was as gentle as could be. Anyway, I got her into there and I aim toward the painting, and then I retire in the corner. After a while the admiral got impatient, and he said, "Well, say something." She didn't say anything. "Well, what have you got to say?" She didn't say anything. There was a wooden arm on this wheelchair. She takes her lorgnette she started tapping on the arm. I think that was a signal for me--I'm quite sure it was--but I wasn't going to respond. I was getting my back up like I did when she called me "Mr. Thingamajig." So finally I decided I had better say something, because the lens will fall out of the lorgnette next, and there is concrete floor, and there was no use letting that break. She was pounding it so hard.

I said, "Do you mean me, Mrs. Kalbfus?"

She said, "Well, who else?"

So I said, "I am sorry, excuse me."

And she said, "Mr. Painter," (now it's Mr. Painter instead of Mr. Thingamajig), "I think it's too . . ."

The admiral looked at me as if to say, "Well, I don't know what too means." He said to her, "Well, would you qualify that--too what?"

And she said, "It's just too . . ."

So he said, "Come on, wheel her out." I never to this day figured out how to evaluate that one. So we wheeled her out and repeated the same episode with the elevator at each level, and then he carried her into the car. When I told Admiral Hart about this on the next telephone communication, he said, "All right, Al, now we've got to take Dutch in tow. I've seen that, and I think it is terrific of him. You did just right; you would have missed the boat if you didn't do these things that you did. So here is what I want you to do. Line up all the General Board's portraits, and we are all coming over there and we aren't going to pay any attention to ours. We are going to look right at his, only at his, and we are going to go right after him and take him in tow. Don't you be upset with anything we say, but we are going to bring him to heel."

Well, I had my boss over there, Lovette, Leland P. Lovette, and I had some trouble with Lovette to support me.* You see, this is where we get back again to Miller on that thing. While I was doing these portraits, they said, "You know this is going to look good right over our mantel at home." And now, in this meeting, all the General Board is in there, all the heavy brass in the Navy. So they were talking about how each one was going to have a separate and special place at home where he was going to hang this.

I said, "Gentlemen, none of this conversation has been addressed to me [I'm over in the corner], but I feel somewhat involved, and the way this hits me..."--and there is my boss standing there who didn't say a darn thing when

---
*Captain Leland P. Lovette, USN, was the Navy's Director of Public Relations during the first part of World War II.

A. K. Murray #1 - 72

I thought, now is the time for him to sound off. And when he didn't, I sounded off.

Q: He was a uniformed Navy man, your boss?

Commander Murray: I was in uniform; we were all in uniform. I don't know what you mean by that.

Q: Lovette--what was his rank?

Commander Murray: He was captain at the time, but he was my boss and it was his place, at this point, to say something. But since he didn't, I thought I had better set the record straight. So I said, "From what I have just heard, it is not different from what I could expect to hear at the Metropolitan Museum if the board of trustees were having a meeting there and were about to adjourn and said, "You know, we have served this institution well, and each of us has so many thousands of pictures and paintings in here. And each of us must have a favorite we like, and having served it so faithfully long, I think it is fitting that each of us take home the one that we have such a fancy for." I said, "If the press was exposed to that, I am sure they would brand it as grand larceny, and I can see no difference in the counterpart of what I am saying and what

I have just heard." Gee, you could have heard a pin drop. Lovette sort of glanced at me, and Hart is about to explode with laughter, but none of the others think it is funny. As they filed out, Hart turned to me and he said, "Murray, you sure sounded off out of turn, but when the heat is on I'm on your side. You can count on me all the way."

But before they got to filing out, they started in on Kalbfus and they said, "Gee, Dutch, you know it's a shame. You spent so much darn money on all that beer that you've drunk to get a belly like you've got on there. Look what you could have bought, a couple of new cars and a grand piano or something else with what you've spent on beer. Look what it's done to you. God, what a paunch you've got." And then they said, "You can't even keep your knees together with that great big wad there." Then they said, "When was the last time you used a hairbrush and a comb? All you use is a damp rag. Of all the bunks you have been on every time you went to sea, were they so short that you rubbed your head on the bulkhead? How did you get rid of all that hair?" They could be abusive and brutal to him.

Q: This was a cruel going-over.

Commander Murray: Then they said, "When was the last time you saw your necktie? The knot is lost up under all those chins. You don't have any neck; it's buried up under there. How do you manage to tie your necktie anyhow?" They really went after him. He didn't get mad. These fellows were kids that he had grown up with, all through his whole professional life, so he didn't take any resentment to it at all. He sort of thawed out; it was a remarkable way for him to react, it seemed to me. I was still over there in the corner and before they went out, he came rolling over toward me and he said, "Murray, I think I did you an injustice; I want to shake your hand." Admiral Hart looked over to me as much as to say, "Well, that's a job well done, isn't it?" So then, out they went.

There is another one about Kalbfus I want to mention. That covers another Hart episode, and it makes sort of human beings out of these fellows too. There is another comical thing that happened in that studio, involving Admiral Nimitz that I might throw in at this time.

Admiral Nimitz was another officer that somehow he and I hit it off, and we became darn good friends. When he had retired and went out to California to live--we had lived in California and I had gone to school in Alameda, right across the bay from where he lived in Berkeley. And he was such an old shoe, a marvelous sort of fellow, and she was so nice, and the children were so nice and everybody was always just great to me. I thought the world of the Nimitzes and the whole family and everything else. There were many little homey touches in that man. One day he was visiting with his daughter down in San Diego when I was doing one of the Marine generals' portraits over there at the Marine base in San Diego, and it was a holiday of some sort. I had just finished my income tax, and his daughter invited the admiral to this holiday dinner. It seems to me it was Thanksgiving, but it couldn't be for income tax.

Q: More likely Easter.

Commander Murray: Maybe that was it. At any rate, Admiral Nimitz was going to come to dinner. He was already there. They got a car for me.

Q: Was this Catherine or Nancy?

Commander Murray: Catherine, she was married to this captain who was down in the boondocks there.

Q: Jimmy Lay.*

Commander Murray: And that is where the meal was to be, and that is where I was invited. He gave me directions as to how to get there, but it was way to the heck and gone out in the brush there. This is in the days when San Diego was way out in the cactus and sagebrush. This driver got

---

*Captain James T. Lay, USN.

A. K. Murray #1 - 76

lost, so we went into a garage there and I went to the telephone. I brought my income tax over to mail. I called the admiral, and he said, "All right, I think I know where you are, but instead of trying to give you instructions on how to get here, you just stay where you are. You can send the driver back and I'll pick you up there. I've got this coupe." He arrived in an old coupe that was so old and so beat up--in those days, you know, you just didn't have any decent kind of a vehicle, and rubber tires were worth more than diamonds. They were the most valuable commodity you could get, and gas was on ration and everything.

I don't know where this car got dredged up from, but the springs were right up through the upholstery and boosted you from the rear. And here was this fleet admiral in there on the one side--you practically had to hold the door to keep it from flying open, the hardware would hardly hold it. Boy, it was something. But he was down driving it. Well, he picked me up. Now I've got this story loused up. Here's the way it was. Now I've got it straight, I guess. When we got there, I had a strange look on my face at this dinner, and he said, "What's the matter, Al?"

And I said, "I just remembered that I don't have the income tax. I'm sure I left it at that telephone in the garage where I called you."

"Ah," he said, "I know how you feel." He turned to Catherine and he said, "Just excuse us, we'll be back in a little while." So then we came out and got into that awful jalopy and drove to that garage. Sure enough, right by the telephone there the darn thing was. So we went out and to the nearest mailbox so he said, "Get rid of it," and down it went. Only somebody that homey, kind fellow would do something like that. Here was this fleet admiral and this crazy lieutenant that goofed like that and he would be that humble and modest and everything.

Back to the time I was with my mother, showing her Alameda again 40 years later, I called on the Nimitzes and they said, "You've got to spend the afternoon; come over for lunch and spend the afternoon with us."

Q: They were in Berkeley then?

Commander Murray: Yes. So we went over there; he had raised some hydrangeas that were marvelous. They were huge, big things, and he was very proud of them. We went out a side door, and down some steps to look at those. They were flagstone steps with a little iron railing. Mother was very frail and quite small; he had a number 12 shoe, a great big foot and he must have weighed about 180 at the time. And he was leading the way, but he lost his footing on the way down, and immediately behind him was Mother. He went down but not too fast, pressed her down too, and I went down behind her. But I realized what was happening, so I got my hand under her pelvis. She was about 80-some, and I was afraid something was going to break, especially with the admiral on top of her. But they were both laughing. They went down so easy that she didn't break anything. The admiral was horrified, but I couldn't get him off, because I was sort of pinned under with her, and he managed to grasp onto the grating and hoisted himself off. Then he turned around to get her off, then I got up. Then we take stock of everybody, and nobody broke anything, so we were all greatly relieved. He was always doing kind things and so was she. When I was doing some business over there on Goat Island (Treasure Island we call it) . . .

Q: Yerba Buena.

Commander Murray: That's exactly it. She used to call over, and she'd say, "Al, what are you doing tonight, Chester is down in Coronado, and Mary and I just made some corn chowder. Would you like some corn chowder? And I've made some garlic bread."

"Oh, I'd love it."

And she'd say, "All right, get a car out of the pool and come on over; it's just Mary and me." So I would go over and get that corn chowder. It was just great. I had marvelous times with her.

Another little episode about the admiral. Admiral Hart was telling me this story. It seems that Hart was going through there, and he paid the admiral a visit. Admiral Nimitz was named to the board of overseers for the Educational System of the State of California. I think they had about 15--quite a number of them in this group. And Admiral Hart asked him, "How are you making out with this educational go-round that you are in? How are you doing on the board?"

Admiral Nimitz said, "I am the board." Now both Admiral Hart and I know that is so out of character, because Nimitz is about as modest a fellow as you would ever dream up, and it isn't what it sounds like when he said, "I am the board."

Q: "The State is I--c'est moi."

Commander Murray: He said, "Let me explain about what I mean. When I came on that thing, for the first meeting I went to I think there were probably 13, they were all there, the next time I came there were only 12, the next time 11, and on down. And now when I come, I am the only one there, I do all the work, that's why I say 'I am the board'. That's what I mean."

Interview Number 2 with Commander Albert K. Murray,
        U.S. Naval Reserve (Retired)

Place: Commander Murray's residence in New York City

Date: Monday, 1 December 1980

Interviewer: John T. Mason, Jr.

Q: Today you were talking off tape for a few minutes about what you intend to convey in terms of the individuals whom you have painted; insight into the person himself or the lady whom you paint; something that, from the artist's point of view, the incisive mind, would feel is a contribution to any biographer who attempts to write the life story of the individual. Is that not right?

Commander Murray: What I was generalizing about was that any data I can get that help to get a better feel for the subject--in my case, the sitter for the painting, and in the historian's case, the subject of his written word or the spoken word. I want anything that reveals a little bit more about him, and these things can be interpreted, plus or minus, by a sensitive reader or overlooked entirely by the insensitive one. In this painting thing you are always, as soon as the subject comes through the door and before that by whatever information you can get, you are constantly having your radar turned on to pick up any kind

A. K. Murray #2 - 81

of nuance that can give you a little better response to what the fellow is about with the hope that the net of this will somehow come off the end of the brush in some way or other that it will be evident to those that are perceptive when they are seeing the finished work.

Many of these comments would be almost of a facetious nature or of a seemingly sidetrack episode. Very often they reveal a sense of humor, or a lack of it, or a short temper, or a phlegmatic disposition--no end of different kinds of things that help to get a little better feel for what the subject or the person is all about. Many of these little episodes that may occur to me may seem almost irrelevant, but to me they have been useful in getting what I think was a closer feel for what the fellow was all about.

Q: Well, indeed, Al, they focus on the man himself, the person as you came to know him, whereas the historian might offhand be interested in the man as he was involved in a certain episode, that sort of thing.

Commander Murray: There is a distinction there all right. However, in that respect, his reaction to these episodes is often predicated on these various other things that I am talking about, and that is how we get the net result out of the end of the tube. It all goes into the one; only

A. K. Murray #2 - 82

certain things come out, but they all have their imprints.

Q: In other words, you are going to provide sort of a basic understanding of this man, and this should be useful to the historian if he has it in time?

Commander Murray: That is the only explanation as to why some of these things are tossed in here.

Q: Now, are we going to talk about Admiral Spruance?

Commander Murray: All right, we might as well. One problem I'll have with these things is, when I get on these various officers, other episodes and officers occur to me, because this is strictly ad lib, as it were.

Q: Don't let that worry you. You expressed this thought the last time, and I tried to reassure you and say that when it is all transcribed it will be indexed, so there is a cross-reference to it.

Commander Murray: I might add this for what it is worth, on this same subject. I was doing James Forrestal's portrait, our first Secretary of Defense. He came over from Secretary of the Navy and was now Secretary of Defense, when that department was formed. He took with him an awful lot of people out of the Navy; one was his secretary, Kate Foley.* Another was Chief Yeoman Cutcomb, plus his entire galley.** Cutcomb I bring up now, because in regard to what we are talking about, Forrestal would often start dictating while he was sitting for me. He kept intensive diaries; every time he would be out at night, the next morning he would get Cutcomb in and write a resume of what took place, who was there, and what he thought of each one and how he evaluated what was said. It was a very confidential business, but then he would start off dictating letters to Cutcomb, and this is the part that made me hold Cutcomb in highest regard.

The dictation might go on for half an hour, but apparently he started off with paragraph one and before you know it, he has slipped into something else, or maybe he has gone down to paragraph five and suddenly new ideas occur to him that obviously don't belong here. They belong somewhere else or probably with paragraph one. No instruction to Cutcomb about anything, and after he rambles on like that for half an hour or so and Cutcomb has got all of this stuff down, he'll take it out. And in about another half hour, he comes in with the letter prepared for the Secretary's signature, and invariably Forrestal would sign without any revisions in it. It always mystified me

---
*Katherine Starr Foley, Forrestal's personal secretary.
**Chief Yeoman Jack E. Cutcomb, USN. Cutcomb later became a warrant officer.

how Cutcomb could get the whole gist of what exactly what was on the Secretary's mind and how he wanted to express it. He got everything in place just right almost on a one-shot basis, but he did it time after time. He was a genius at that sort of thing.

Well, I just jump all over the place here without any indication. I start off with Admiral Spruance here, but it brings to mind something about Admiral Nimitz next, and so on, but at least I try to put a parenthetical asterisk here.

Back to Spruance; he is one of the most modest of men that I have met in my entire life--totally self-effacing. And while he was a giant in all respects, he had a rather frail, almost a feminine voice and anything but a desk-pounding, high-powered, 100-octane kind of impression to give people, and yet he was all of that inside. He was a man of steel but tempered with extreme sensitivity, marvelous judgment, kindness, and a perfectly terrific individual--one of the most impressive and inspiring men that I ever have had the privilege of knowing. But there were little characteristics of his that were both amusing and instructive. One of them was, he disliked abuse of his time by thoughtless people. At the war college he wouldn't have a desk.* He did his work standing at a pulpit to discourage anyone to come in and shoot the breeze come 4:00

---
*Admiral Raymond A. Spruance, USN, served as president of the Naval War College from 1 March 1946 to 1 July 1948.

o'clock or something else.

Q: And they would have to stand too?

Commander Murray: Yes, there were no chairs for them to sit down, so that helped out that situation a little bit. Then, another thing, he used to like to go swimming every afternoon, and this operation of the painting took place during the Thanksgiving period, and we were swimming in the ocean. And up there in Newport it would be in the low 50s; it would be awfully darn cold. I first stayed in the BOQ, but he ordered me over to his quarters, because they had a little fully fixed up place up on the third deck, so I was up there.*

We would go swimming every afternoon.

Q: This was the duty of the artist also?

Commander Murray: Well, I felt it was, and I liked to swim too but not in November in the Atlantic Ocean, especially up in New England. We would get into our bathing suits in his car and drive over there. This was a time when there were running boards on the automobiles, and we would have a bucket. There wouldn't be water in it yet--and towels, so we wrapped ourselves up in towels over our bathing suits

---

*BOQ--bachelor officers' quarters.

and drove off to the beach. The place we went to was Third Beach, which was out on the end of a horseshoe. It was three-quarters of a mile from the end of that horseshoe to the other side. Once you got in there was nothing to do but fight it out until you got to the other side.

By the way, I am not a bad swimmer, but I am not a good one either. However, I could never keep up with the admiral. He was always considerably ahead of me and if I was fortunate enough to finally catch up with him, I accused him once of having an outboard motor in his swimming pants because he was always so far ahead. He was 20 or more years my senior, and I felt I had to do this, and I was embarrassed that I couldn't keep up with him.* When we got to the other side, practically purple with cold, the next thing you had to do was jog around the beach, back to where the car was, in order to evaporate the water and dry off a little bit.

Q: And get the circulation back.

Commander Murray: That happened incidentally, but the main thing was to not put too much water on the upholstery of the car. Once we got back there, then we dried off vigorously and then sat on whatever was left of the towel that wasn't too wet. But after that we filled the bucket

---

*Spruance was born in 1886, Murray in 1906.

with seawater and rinsed the sand off our feet and then dried them off and got in the car, to keep the sand out of the car. Then we threw the water out, put the bucket in, and drove back to the war college.

This routine developed--he'd been doing that as a much younger officer. He had been there in Newport with his young family. He did the same thing, about the sand and the bucket of water, but he found the children didn't like it; they were embarrassed that he should do that. He was using common sense, because he hated to have to sweep the sand off the floorboards of the automobile all the time, and this was one way to stop it--very common sense but the children took offense to it, because they thought it was rather stuffy or some other kind of thing. Rather than try to exert parental influence, he simply knocked it off with them and didn't do it.

He was constantly doing these things, when people that he was close to had some objections or something, he would back off and be extremely considerate. He was remarkably that way with his wife. They had a wonderful thing going every day of their married life which he had great talent for to bring these things about. On those swimming episodes he liked Meyers Rum, a dark rum, and that was one big reward for the paralyzing flagellation that went on every time we did this. He introduced me to this terrific drink; I'm not much of a drinking man, but I thought this was superb. It was a jigger of Meyers Rum first in a glass that had about half an inch of syrupy sugar water, if you like the drink fairly sweet, with some lime juice. Then he put in this jigger of rum, and then he filled up this big highball glass with sherry. If it was a bitter cold day, that would be heated. If it was not so cold, it would have a little ice in it or at room temperature. However you had it, temperature-wise, it was one of the niftiest things that I ever put down. If it was quite a successful afternoon, we would have two of those, but it was really something.

Q: Did you continue to paint after that?

Commander Murray: It wasn't that powerful. It just really got things going again after this traumatic episode of the swimming. The other thing about libation in his house, he had been very famous for a coffee that he brewed in his house. I had been importuned about this, and I thought I would pull a leg a little bit. So the first morning I came down for breakfast, he was sitting there in a bathrobe and he poured me a cup of this coffee that he had just brewed, that I had heard all about but never had had before. So I deliberately didn't say anything after I took a great big drink of it, and he was looking at me waiting for me to say something. I didn't say anything on purpose. Then I drank another one, and he said, "Let me put some more in it and fill it up." So I let him fill it up, but now he can't understand why I am not making some enthusiastic comment.

Finally, after I drank this again, I said, "There is just one thing wrong with this, Admiral." Gee, he was shocked, and finally I said, "The trouble is, anything that is as absolutely divine as this, a nectar like this is for the gods; you ought to be in ceremonial robes not that bathrobe." His eyebrows shot back into normal position again, and he smiled, and God was back in his heaven.

Q: It was Hawaiian coffee basically, wasn't it?

Commander Murray: Yes, it came from the Kona Coast. He used to buy it there from Magruder in Washington, mixed in with another type of Magruder's coffee.* Then he had one of those great big old country store grinders like you might have seen in a grocery store when you were a kid, with about a three-foot diameter wheel and the groceryman grinds up your coffee. He had one of those and he would hand-grind this stuff, and it was a very good coffee, marvelous. They had a lot of them in the Marine Corps, as you may know.

The admiral also had a little schnauzer dog that

---
*Magruder's is a grocery store chain in the Washington, D.C., area.

adored him, but he was a first-class milquetoast. I think the dog suspected that the admiral knew this, but he was trying his best to ignore it or hoped to convey another impression. I was importuned about this characteristic of the dog when we used to take walks after the swimming or maybe before dinner. We would have a little walk around the war college there, and he would have this schnauzer. One day we were doing this when a cat appeared; this cat was well-known to the schnauzer and to the admiral, but it was not about to be intimidated by this dog. It had the number on the dog and the dog knew it.

The admiral and I both saw the cat at about the same time the dog did and he took a quick look to see if the admiral had seen it and came to the conclusion that he hadn't, so now the dog is trying to ignore the presence of the cat over near a pole. The admiral is heading toward the pole in order to force the dog to recognize the cat; he knows darn well the dog saw the cat. So they get up by the pole and the dog can't stand any longer making believe he doesn't see that the cat is there, so he looks directly at the cat and starts to rush up to challenge the cat, expecting the cat to go up the tree.

All this little scene is exactly what the admiral wanted, just to show me exactly what a sissy this dog really was. The dog rushes up to the cat and the cat stood its ground, the dog--if you could have the sound effects as in the movies, there is a terrible screech of rubber as the dog is trying to come to a halt and to get into reverse at the same time. He can't quite make it, and the cat hits him on the end of the nose with his paw. There is a scream from the dog, and he backs off and starts to run back toward the admiral. The admiral calls his name out sharply. He then turns around once more and makes a feeble rush toward the cat. The cat hits him once more and then leisurely goes up the tree and sits on a branch. So then we turned and walked back toward the building, and the admiral said, "You see what I mean, he thought he could get away with this; he tries it frequently with me. I usually see what he sees at about the same time and maybe even before he does." This is one of those amusing little quirks that we ran into constantly with the admiral.

During my time there, Admiral Nimitz was asked to come over to address the Admiralty in London about the Marianas campaign or about something in the Pacific--I don't believe it was the Marianas at that time. It was not possible for Admiral Nimitz to go--he was then CNO--and he asked Raymond Spruance to go. I don't recall the aide's last name--Sam was his first name, a charming young fellow, a senior lieutenant. They were gone about three days. When they came back, walking through the door, Mrs. Spruance said, "Well, Raymond how did they receive you over there?" He, in his usual way, just shrugged his shoulders and made a grimace on his face with no comment.

Sam reached in his pocket and pulled out a large, folded-up part of the London *Times* and *Manchester Guardian* and signalled to Mrs. Spruance that he had all the data. It turned out that about half of the front page of the *Times* and a large section of the other paper--on the front page, not buried somewhere in the back--this remarkable address that Admiral Spruance had given that had everybody on the edge of their chairs. But the admiral wasn't even going to show it to his wife or anybody else; he didn't even know he had it, he didn't cut out anything himself; Sam did it. This is typical of Admiral Spruance's modesty; he was always low-pedaling himself.

In the Pacific at one point there, he had on board Holland Smith (called by the press "Howling Mad" Smith) of the Marine Corps, and Richmond Kelly Turner, the amphibious commander at the time in this area.* These two officers were having a bellicose time about where to deploy the Marines in this campaign. They said they were shouting so that you could hear them clear back in Washington.

Suddenly they were summoned to Admiral Spruance's cabin; they were on his flagship. So he said, "Sit down

---

*This may have been during the Marianas campaign in the spring of 1944. Admiral Spruance was Commander Fifth Fleet. Lieutenant General Holland M. Smith, USMC, was the landing force commander, and Vice Admiral Richmond K. Turner, USN, was commander of the amphibious task force.

gentlemen. I hear this discussion going on. I would like to hear from both of you. Holland, we will start with you. Where do you want the Marines deployed?" So then he heard what General Smith had to say. Then he turned to Turner and he said, "Well, Kelly, what do you want to do about this?" And he told him what he wanted. So, in his high-pitched, quiet, judicial voice, Spruance said, "Well, the Marines will be deployed so-and-so. Good day, gentlemen."

That just stopped all this yelling and table pounding and bellicose screaming that had been going on between the two fellows down in their quarters. This was typical of that quiet, authoritative way that he would do things and lay down the law. That's that and no one would question what he was doing, because nine times out of ten he was extremely correct and sound.

Q: Was he a willing subject when you painted him?

Commander Murray: Yes, he was. I felt of him as being 11 or 12 feet tall and he was, as I recall, probably about 5 feet 9 inches or thereabouts. I wanted a bigger figure, standing. First I asked him, too, would he warm up to having others in this with him, his staff or something. He thought that would be great; he always liked to share everything with everybody if it's ever a tribute or anything of that nature. It wound up that we had Carl

Admiral Raymond A. Spruance and staff

Moore as his chief of staff, and Forrestel, and Biggs.*

What I contrived was a deck scene with the admiral conferring with his officers there; they were looking at a large chart. Admiral Spruance was uncovered; there was a sailor about to raise a signal hoist behind them, as though a decision would be made here. Other ships in line would be informed of it with the signal hoist of executing some maneuver or whatever it was that was to take place as a result of this deckside conference, and I had the ship on rather a sharp list, as in a turn or something in order to put Admiral Spruance on the top end of the seesaw on this in order to give him height. This was a technical thing that I was doing in order to have him dominate this thing physically.

Q: As I recall, you succeeded very well, because he is the dominant figure.

Commander Murray: That is the explanation of how I was trying to accomplish that. On that same score about how these people look and why I would do things of this nature, now I will jump to Admiral King.

As you may recall, he was quite bald-headed, and he was not a commanding, imposing appearing fellow in the

---

*Captain Charles J. ("Carl") Moore, USN, Fifth Fleet chief of staff; Captain Emmet P. Forrestel, USN, Fifth Fleet operations officer; Captain Burton B. Biggs, USN, Fifth Fleet logistics officer.

Fleet Admiral Ernest J. King

pictorial sense of his head or his physique, like for instance William F. Halsey was. Halsey had a face sort of hammered out of steel or like the old craggy one of the "old man of the mountain" in New Hampshire. King had rather an austere look, but the bald head didn't give him the pizzazz that pictorially helped out Halsey. Since he was the Commander in Chief of the Navy, the greatest Navy we ever had, I wanted a feeling of immense authority here. I was thinking of the mace that the Lord Mayor of London would carry in his hand on ceremonial things, which gives him the dignity and power of office. People aren't going to overlook this thing, it is a symbol that carried enormous weight.

Q: Threatening too.

Commander Murray: Yes, if necessary. So I had him covered with his cap. And, having been an enlisted man at one point, I well know that the officer's insignia on a cap is something like a mace in the Lord Mayor's hand on ceremonial affairs. It is a rather commanding symbol of authority, unquestioned authority, so that this device on his cap was a more than ample head of hair in the sense of giving him whatever was needed to let people know loud and clear that this was the Commander in Chief. However, as a fleet admiral there is an immense amount of gold braid on the sleeves and I didn't want to be competitive with the head.

Your eye often plays tricks as an observer, so you need to kill and put in a subordinate role those things that would be competitive with the primary target in regard to this gold braid. So I threw the uniform raincoat over one arm which covered up a large part of the gold braid that showed on the other sleeve, but it helped to minimize the competition with the ribbons on his breast and show the interest up to the primary target on the head. These things I am constantly doing in one way or another to make the observer see the things that you want them to see, much like the stage electrician does with the people under the proscenium arch to get them to see what they want to see when they want to see it.

Q: As I recall King in the corridors of the Navy Department with all that gold braid on his arms, it made the arms look elongated and out of proportion actually.

Commander Murray: Well, he did have long arms. He was a pretty long, thin fellow, but that gold braid can often be so attractive to the eye that the observer would see that first, which would be a disaster. We ought to collide with the individual first and finally get to the gold braid.

Q: Did he understand what you were trying to accomplish by having him with this?

Commander Murray: Yes, he didn't feel that I was slighting anything that he had spent a lifetime to gain and earn and be recognized for. But I was also aware of other things, like the wings that he wore; those were out from under his lapel. Most naval aviators hold those in high esteem; they worked hard for those little gold wings that are on their uniform. The blue uniform lapel very often would cover half of it and more. We moved the wings out so that they became much more evident for the layman to know exactly what they were. I would try to give them their full due on these things that were significant to them.

Q: When was it that you painted King, approximately?

Commander Murray: That's another little interesting thing. Operation Olympic, as you may recall, was the code name for the actual invasion of Japan which never took place, thanks to the atomic bombs on Hiroshima and Nagasaki.* On New Year's day that year, I had orders to go over to the fleet for that assault on Japan. As I was standing on the runway

---
*B-29 bombers of the U.S. Army Air Forces dropped atomic bombs on Hiroshima, Japan, on 6 August 1945 and on Nagasaki, Japan, on 9 August 1945. The Japanese surrendered shortly afterward.

over at the MATS terminal there to go, a Jeep came roaring up and said, "Are you Commander Murray?"*

"Yes."

He said, "Well, your orders are canceled. Get aboard. Admiral King wants to see you right now."

So I said to myself, "What in the world is going on? I thought this was going to be the coup de grace, the final thing, the close of the war. If the admiral wants me to paint his portrait now, there's plenty of things I don't know anything about. This must be on ice if that's the case." So, sure enough, he was quartered in a little bedroom and bathroom stuffed right over the Main Navy entrance on Constitution Avenue. So I went up there and that is what we arranged then--the sittings which began the next day.

Q: No explanation as to why?

Commander Murray: No. Of course, we didn't have to have that operation. Incidentally, the perfidy of the Russians had always galled me. They had been importuned two months before they did anything, to intercede on what terms the Allies would accept peace from Japan, and they let two months go by. Prince Konoye had importuned them to do this

---
*MATS--Military Air Transport Service, then a part of the U.S. Army Air Forces, since renamed Military Airlift Command.

and after the two months the Russians became convinced that the Japs really were finished.*

If they wanted to get in on the spoils, they had to become belligerents. So, never saying anything to the Allies, they became belligerents. If ever there was a double-cross of humanity, it seems to me that was it. Now they are betting on a sure thing and they let further carnage go on on both sides, all of which could have been stopped if the Russians had done as they were asked to do. That gave them their foot in the door, and they were now on the team of the victors. Little is ever made of that; we don't ever seem to throw it back at the Russians or tell the third nations people, "Look, this is another one of the large inventory of double-crosses that those people are constantly making at top level." Well, at any rate, that's another digression.

On the score of other things about Admiral King, he did have a sense of humor, quite a good one. He was also sensitive in ways that many people thought he wouldn't be. He had announced to the press when he was first assigned as Chief of Naval Operations, our number one in the Navy for that war, that, "Somebody has got to be an SOB, and I am telling you fellows in the press right now so you will know, loud and clear, it is me; I will be that fellow." He was also quite thoughtful. In that respect, shortly after

---

*Prince Fumimaro Konoye, cousin of Emperor Hirohito; Japanese premier prior to World War II.

we began this painting he said to me, "Did you ever read Booth Tarkington?"

I said, "Sure, but I read him an awful long time ago." He didn't say anything further about it. The next day when he came in he handed me a small volume called Rumbin Galleries, by Booth Tarkington. It was a wonderful love story about an art dealer down here in Greenwich Village in New York. It had a rather tired out binding and I opened it up, and in the back there was a District of Columbia Library, Ernest J. King card there in the envelope and the library stamp. I assumed that he didn't go over in the stacks and get it, his aide probably did, but he only did it on the instructions of his boss.

I thought, "Well, by God this man can't be all that tough if he is going to be that sensitive to an artist here, and he is thinking, 'What might I do that will please this fellow?'" So he goes and gets this book, which impresses quite forcefully with me the feeling that this man isn't all that tough and severe; he is quite thoughtful in many respects. Painting the thing got dragged out terribly, but before we got through he had to make a rather rush trip out to Seattle and flying out there, they were at about 11,000 feet and were going to have to go higher. The oxygen supply broke down. The admiral had some kind of a heart attack or drastic stroke. He came back with loss of speech.

A. K. Murray #2 - 101

Q: This was in 1945?

Commander Murray: Yes.* He had to write everything out. He had a little pad and pencil; speaking was extremely difficult, and the words were so garbled you couldn't understand what he was saying. So he would communicate with this pencil and paper. We seemed to have an affinity. I used to go and see him frequently after the war was over when he was living on the 17th floor of Bethesda Hospital. He couldn't be more pleased any time I would show up there. It was a very monastic kind of existence; there was just the bed and the wash basin and a chiffonier or bureau there. That was apparently all he wanted, and that was all he had.

His family had tried to get him to come back with them; he had had eight children, all daughters except one boy, Ernest.** He had had an unhappy time in married life, and he chose not to go back, which always rather depressed and shocked me, because he had gone to the summit in achievements in his profession and in the world history. There never had been a navy like the United States Navy, and he had been the head of it. He and Admiral Nimitz were the two great giants of the whole thing, and yet he wouldn't go back to close out his remaining years with his

---
*According to King's biography, <u>Master of Sea Power</u> by Thomas Buell, the first stroke was in 1947 and others followed later.
**King and his wife had six daughters and a son.

family. He instead chose to live in this monastic existence out there at the Bethesda Hospital. Maybe that was one of the reasons he was so glad to see somebody once in a while. I got so warmly received each time I would go pay him a little visit.

Q: How long did it take him to overcome the difficulty in 1945?

Commander Murray: I think he did fairly well with it. I don't remember now, 30-odd years later, how long it did take him, but he did make quite a substantial recovery, a remarkable recovery. He wasn't handicapped to any degree with locomotion either; his hands and feet seemed to cooperate and behave fairly well. Speech was the main thing; his mind was clear.

Q: How long did it take you to complete your painting?

Commander Murray: That one I am not clear about either at this time. We did, of course, finish after this thing had occurred, but it didn't have any deleterious effects in the appearance of it or in his effectiveness of cooperating for what was required of him.

A. K. Murray #2 - 103

Q: We'll switch to Admiral Nimitz, and this is also about that time, was it--1946, something like that?

Commander Murray: Yes, this is when Nimitz was Chief of Naval Operations. I was trying to do this thing at the climax of Admiral Nimitz's career, which had been symbolized by the signing of the peace treaty aboard the Missouri.* The scene however would be Admiral Nimitz's portrait; he would be the central figure, so I envisioned this whole thing from the collections of photos and all that were in abundance of that episode in Tokyo Bay when the issue took place. I set up a table on which the peace document would be with the Allies in attendance, the entire group of those, and the Japanese contingent with Shigemitsu and Umezu and the rest of them over on the other side of the ship.** I moved this whole business from the starboard to the port side in order to get an effect on the deck, of gun barrels of forward gun mounts on this forward deck where the ceremony took place.

By doing this, I could have the sunshine make shadows from those gun barrels that looked like the Japanese naval ensign on the deck on which everybody was standing. So here we have a maritime nation that had darned near

---

*Admiral Nimitz signed the surrender document on behalf of the United States in a ceremony on board the battleship Missouri in Tokyo Bay on 2 September 1945.
**Mamoru Shigemitsu, Japanese Foreign Minister; General Yoshijiro, Chief of the Army General Staff.

Fleet Admiral Chester W. Nimitz

succeeded in being number one in the maritime world but finally was destroyed by the combined might of the various nations now all present. All of them were now standing on the symbolized thing of the Japanese naval ensign. That was just one little digression of why I put the thing over on the port side.

Q: This was done in the Corcoran studio?

Commander Murray: In the Corcoran studio, yes, where they had marvelous light.* And so the admiral is in his khakis, open shirt and the collar and the whole business. And I reassembled a composition that would include the entire Allied contingent behind Admiral Nimitz who had just signed the document for the United States, and he was rising from his chair.

Q: How did you handle MacArthur?

Commander Murray: Behind Admiral Nimitz was MacArthur, and he would be the next signator, and he is wearing his campaign hat while Admiral Nimitz is uncovered and his cap is on the table. Behind them are Lord Fraser for the

---

*Corcoran Gallery of Art, 17th Street and New York Avenue in Washington, D.C.

British, Helfrich for the Dutch, Leclerc for the French, and right on down the list.* I'd have to refresh my memory. Then over on the other side were the whole Japanese contingent and in front, in tailcoat and striped trousers, was Shigemitsu.

So now we are doing that in the Corcoran. There was an assistant director there by the name of John Leeper.** He and I became good friends. This was in the summertime. I was in a khaki uniform, as the admiral was too. I had a date to start painting at about 12:30 with the admiral. Around 11:30 Leeper came along and said, "Look, this is a hot summer day; let's have lunch." Right up the street was a little place that had Michelob, a draft beer. So I thought, "That would be a nice idea on this hot summer day, and one beer wouldn't be a bad thing."

So we went up there and I was aware that Leeper had a sadistic twist to him at times, but it never dawned on me at this time to pay attention to it. We didn't get this beer until we were nearly through with the meal, and when it was brought in, the rascal contrived to deliberately knock my glass right into my lap, so now I had a dark wet stain on the front of my trousers. And I had to walk down the sidewalk back to the Corcoran in a uniform that looked

---

*Admiral Sir Bruce Fraser, RN, Commander in Chief, British Pacific Fleet; Admiral Conrad E.L. Helfrich, Commander of Netherlands naval forces in the Far East; General Jacques P. Leclerc, Free French forces.
**John P. Leeper, assistant director.

like I should first rush to my urologist to find out what was the matter. Leeper was beside himself with glee for his achievement; he thought that was the funniest darn thing.

I was concerned about how in the world I was going to get down the sidewalk, because it would be loaded now with personnel. It was now approaching 12:30, and everybody would be coming for lunch up from Main Navy, and that place would be loaded with Navy and Army officers and I'll have to salute to them all looking like this.* It occurred to me that this cashier, a big tough blonde, the type you might think would be some kind of madam in a brothel or something. She sold newspapers, however. I thought, "I'll get a newspaper and I can just fold that up and hold it in front of me; it was only about a block and a half to the Corcoran.

Q: You were having lunch at the McReynolds probably.

Commander Murray: It was right across from old Main Navy there, the old Army-Navy Building; it is now gone long ago. Unfortunately, she didn't have any; she was sold out. Now there was nothing to do but put my cap on, walk right out bold and brazen, and everybody would be looking at me and

---

*Main Navy--the Navy Department headquarters building at 17th Street and Constitution Avenue.

turning around again; they can't believe what they're seeing. Leeper didn't walk with me; he was about three steps behind laughing like a hyena, thinking he was so clever and funny. I got to the Corcoran, fortunately, and the guard in attendance wondered what had happened to me too.

I went into the studio, which is a great big room, and opened the window to get some air in there and took my trousers off and found the shirttail was all wet too, so I had to take my shirt off. I hung them up on a coat rack and the room began to smell pretty heavily of beer. You may know how it might be if your wife didn't empty some beer glasses of the night before, sort of like cigar butts that are left in. Pretty soon the room smells of cigar butts or old beer. The next day it's pretty bad. That's about the way the studio suddenly became.

Well, the door opened, and in came Admiral Nimitz in his khaki uniform. He sniffed a couple of times and said, "Am I in the Corcoran, or am I in a brewery?" Then I stepped around from behind the painting there and he sees me. I'm in my skivvies. I have socks and shoes, skivvy shorts and top on and that's all. "Well," he said, "what's going on? Do you want me to take my clothes off down to that too?" He was very good-natured about it all, which was typical of him. I apologized and he said, "Oh, I see you've got it all hanging up on the line there," and then I told him what happened. I spent the rest of the afternoon painting the Chief of Naval Operations in my underwear there while my beer-soaked uniform was drying out.

Q: What were you trying to achieve with Nimitz?

Commander Murray: I wanted that scene of the surrender, which would be the climax of his long and exciting career. That would be my whole target and summit. I wanted it to be dominated by him, and I could do that by placing him the way I did, sort of in front of the others at the table where everybody else is more or less behind him as they would normally be in a physical setup of this kind. It is his portrait, but it's in a setting of probably the climax of his naval career.

Q: The Navy man is the top man in that whole picture; is that the thought?

Commander Murray: Oh yes, after all, this was the Pacific War, which essentially was a naval war anyway. Although the Army and the air were tremendously involved, it was really naval warfare for the most part.

Q: Did the general ever comment on this?

Commander Murray: No. He had his day too. I was surprised up there at West Point; I did a portrait up there later of one of the superintendents and found a portrait of MacArthur which was a pretty good one. But so many of them up there never did anything; they were all in the Corps of Engineers, the bulk of them, which rather surprised me. You would think that other branches of the service might have been equally distinguished, but it wasn't so; it wasn't artillery, or infantry, or cavalry. The engineers seemed to be top dogs generation after generation in the hierarchy at the academy.

In this business of painting, sometimes it has been referred to as a psychiatrist's couch. The darndest things come into the conversation. In recent times, when I was doing the portrait of Jimmy Holloway, he referred to me as a shrink, and he felt that he was on the psychiatrist's couch so many times in there, because we would talk about all manner of things. In regard to Admiral Nimitz on this score, being a very distinguished submariner and going way back in submarine types, the old S-types and so on, he asked me if I knew that most all submariners were constipated, especially the more senior ones.

"No, I wasn't apprised of that fact."

He said, "Well, it's quite true, and there is a very reasonable explanation. You know in those early boats we only had two heads, one forward and one aft. We had to keep weight down so there wouldn't be doors. There would be a piece of canvas just thrown over the hopper there, around it. So you were subject to all sorts of ribald remarks from everybody in the crew when you go in there to mount the throne and do your duty. And if there are many sound effects, that produces all sorts of additional remarks from everywhere, so the tendency would be to put this thing off until the very last moment when, hopefully, it could be accomplished with a minimum amount of time required or to reduce the episodes that were bound to occur. Through that practice over the years, almost all submariners become quite constipated and that is why."

Another thing he said, "You know those early boats didn't have very good heat. When we would go out in New London on three-day maneuvers, most of us would bring down The New York Times and the wives would drive us down and we would climb aboard the sub with The New York Times under our arm and we would soon peel off to our skivvies and then put the sections of the Times around us as insulation, then get dressed again with that in there. We would be a little noisy and crisp in our movements for a while, but after a couple of days it was great. It was nice and oily and bent, and by the third day when we were ready to come back it was marvelous. We didn't have any chilly episodes, and it was wonderful insulation, the only bad part was we got a little bit gamey sometimes and our wives would make us sit in the back seat when we got back into the car."

I am really giving you a big business about excerpting these things and putting them in where they belong. This thought just occurred to me about Arleigh Burke and his Little Beaver Squadron in regard to a tendency that I would call sort of "operating by the seat of his pants" as a squadron commander.* He had a sixth sense that endeared him to his men enormously. A sample of it, one night he was complying with Admiral Halsey's orders (his boss). Admiral Halsey would often send him dispatches to intercept the Japs at latitude so-and-so and longitude so-and-so at such and such a time, Admiral Halsey laying his calipers over reefs and atolls and everything else and not taking into consideration that Burke would have to stay in deep water and go all around Robin Hood's Barn to do this. So the response often was, "I am complying as directed; we are making 31 knots,"--(way beyond the specifications of the manufacturer; they should blow up at that point). But he felt obliged to do it in order to stay on schedule; hence he became known as "31-knot Burke."

On one of those nights, around midnight, six destroyers in line and he had a hunch they were under surveillance and ordered a change of course for one minute

---

*Little Beaver Squadron was the nickname of Destroyer Squadron 23, commanded by Captain Arleigh A. Burke, USN, in the Solomons in 1943.

and then to swing back on the original course. They had no sonar contact, no radar contact. As the last destroyer swung out of line, just as it had gotten into its new position, the detonations occurred in the turbulent areas they had just left. Those <u>Fletcher</u>-class destroyers, 2,100 tons, carried about 60,000 horsepower, and that would so churn up the sea that you would have a waterline like a concrete wall right behind where the propellers were. When the torpedoes collided with this, they detonated and that is what occurred just as the last of the destroyers had gotten out of line. The whole crew knew that he had no contact. This was just one of those episodes that he just did "by the seat of his pants," or a hunch, or intuition.

This happened to him time after time, things of a similar nature which would make his men just swear by him. He also had some very good things going for him now and then; like one area that he was to swing into this shore area of Japan, and destroy it by gunfire. When he went by it, though, the circumstances had changed and he didn't have time to go in there, so he simply shelled it as best as he could going by there at high speed. Later on, he encountered the Japanese commander of that area who was aware of the episode. In talking about it with Burke, he said, "You know it is a real good thing you didn't come into our harbor, because that very afternoon we had just completed one of the heaviest mining operations we had ever done. You wouldn't be here today if you had swung in there."

Q: That was down in Rabaul, wasn't it?

Commander Murray: I don't know where the location was, but at any rate that was one of those little things that helped to keep Arleigh with us. Another one: the nature of the man as a seafaring fellow. At one point his squadron sighted a small Japanese vessel that challenged them. The Japanese didn't have a chance and they knew it, but they felt obliged to challenge the U.S. at this point and they were promptly sunk; there were very few survivors. Arleigh cruised around to pick up any survivors that were there, and then they picked up all the bodies that they could, those that were floating around that could be picked up and then had burial at sea for them right on the spot.

The survivors carried that message back to Japan, and some time later one of the most moving experiences that Arleigh Burke ever had was a ceremony he was invited to during one of his returns to Japan, by this community who honored him in the most extraordinary fashion, almost as a demigod for his conduct in making that burial at sea. The ceremony for those people who died knowing they didn't have a chance, but they did what they were expected to do and died doing it. But Burke also respected them for what they did and gave them full honors and full credit, which was what so touched the Japanese, the families and all, and, of course, it touched him deeply that they were that responsive. There was no bitterness or anything else, just deep respect and regard, much as that business of the Bridge Over the River Kwai where the Japanese train was blown up, but the British prisoners rushed to their rescue, as they had both been there.* They had both been badly mauled physically and were desperately injured, so that was the fraternity or denominator that took precedence over all others. They both were suffering from the same thing and they had both been there.

Q: On that occasion, when Arleigh was back in Japan, he was inducted into the Veterans of Rabaul. It was a Shinto ceremony because of this incident that you just described.

Commander Murray: I always marvel at his kind of dual personality, or schizophrenia if you want to call it that. The same thing with O'Kane, the submarine commander.** Arleigh had wonderful friends in Japan, or adversaries; he

---

*Pierre Boulle, The Bridge Over the River Kwai, translated by Xan Fielding (New York: Vanguard Press, 1954). This novel, which was later made into a popular movie, depicted the battle of wits and endurance between a Japanese prisoner camp commander and the senior officer among a group of British prisoners of war.
**Commander Richard H. O'Kane, USN, Medal of Honor recipient whose story is contained in his memoir Clear the Bridge! The War Patrols of the U.S.S. Tang (Chicago: Rand McNally & Company, 1977).

had immense compassion and understanding, far in excess of anything I could ever hope to have. O'Kane was the same way; when those Irish eyes of O'Kane would look in that periscope and order "fire one" and "fire two" of those torpedoes, knowing that in a few moments there would be mayhem beyond description that was going to take place, a horrible carnage. Yet I don't know of a man more kind or sympathetic than O'Kane; he could be both ways. Having travelled with him a lot and gone on camping trips with him to Alaska and around, I couldn't get over that he was always so good about animals and women and children and sympathetic to people in all matters. I would expect him to have a much shorter latitude in these ways. I may have mentioned going by the stockade in southern France when I could have gone off the deep end in a hurry. Well, you see how different it was with me, I didn't have that slack in the line. I am afraid I couldn't forgive them as fast as both Arleigh and O'Kane could.

Q: Arleigh had to be educated a bit; it was an evolvement, as he described it to me. It took him a while, but then he began to see the good traits in the former enemy.

Commander Murray: He has always seen good traits in all adversaries in all phases; that is one of the wonderful things about Arleigh. He can always dig up something awfully interesting about something, where he picks up the little bit of this or that. His radar is always turning around to soak up any kind of useful information, and he had a memory bank that could pull it out when he needed it too.

Q: Still has. Tell me about painting him.

Commander Murray: Well, I wanted a salty affair with this if I could, because he was such a marvelous destroyer commander. You see, we had broken this list down into ship types, and when we got to destroyers he would be at the top of the list, along with Moosbrugger and a very few others that could in any way be equally there to the extent that he was.*

Q: What time frame was this when you were painting?

Commander Murray: He had come back and had just been demoted from commodore to captain when the commodore rank was being taken out.

Q: Was he on the General Board?

---

*Commander Frederick Moosbrugger, USN, Commander Destroyer Division 12. Like Burke, he made a name for himself in the Solomons operations of 1943.

Captain Arleigh A. Burke

A. K. Murray #2 - 117

Commander Murray: No, he was not on the General Board. I don't know what his job was at the time. He was doing a lot of legwork for [unclear]. He went out one time there to the University of New Mexico to straighten out a contract that was getting nowhere with the Navy. The scientific engineering department in New Mexico and the president were not speaking to each other, and the Navy was stalled in the meantime and needed this stuff promptly. So Arleigh went out and he got these two fellows who were at loggerheads together at a breakfast meeting and had them on a first-name basis again, and the Navy got their stuff even ahead of time. The admirals' revolt was about to take place at this same time, when Arleigh was doing most of the legwork, and that is what caused him to be passed over.

Q: He was an officer in OP-23 then.

Commander Murray: I guess that is what he was doing at the time. In regard to this painting, I was envisioning him in presumably a general quarters scene at night aboard his lead destroyer, breaking out of the sack in those little quarters that the commander would have up on the bridge, trying to get what cat naps and rest he could. The illumination by flares, an amber kind of a light from aerial flares. I had a colored fellow there as a talker, helmeted, and they are under attack in a general quarters scene. I had this fellow and Arleigh get into some oilskins as he is trying to rush out of his quarters there and get a firsthand feel for what is happening. That was the way life was aboard that kind of destroyer squadron in those days of heavy duty for everybody right around the clock.

Q: Did you have any difficulty in getting the proper expression on his countenance?

Commander Murray: No. I didn't have that problem with Arleigh Burke that I had had with some of the others.

On two occasions--this is when he was living out there in Hawthorne Place around behind Foxhall Road--somehow we hit it off right from the start. So he was going to have a cookout in the summer. He said, "Come on out and we will have dinner." That was the first night that he had been passed over, and he was very blue. His wife, Bobbie, was very good with the squeeze box as she called the accordion, and she would play salty little numbers and things that we might have had in the old sailing vessel days, along with other numbers that would be good with an accordion. But it was a depressed kind of an evening because poor Arleigh felt so poorly.

A. K. Murray #2 - 119

Q: Just the three of you?

Commander Murray: As I recall. But, the next time, strangely enough, we duplicated this little episode of cooking out in the back and this time he was passed over again, and this time his classmate Freddie Withington made it, and he didn't.* Arleigh said, "I am going to turn in my suit, I've had it."

"No," I said, "Arleigh, the likes of you are too rare in the Navy; you hang on, I wouldn't be at all surprised to see you CNO one time." I wouldn't presume to be a Delphic oracle, but it looks like that is what it turned out to be.**

In the Burke portrait, the fellow with the talker headset on was Charles Lawrence, and he was the messenger that I had at the time when I was running the Combat Art Section. I was doing this portrait of Arleigh Burke, and I wanted a black in this picture and so rigged up my messenger, Charles Lawrence, who later ran the whole thing, and up even to this day as we are talking about it I think is currently running the Combat Art Section. That was his beginning back in those days.

Q: He is the curator or whatever you might call him. Now

---

*Also a member of the class of 1923 at the Naval Academy, Frederic S. Withington was selected for promotion to rear admiral in 1949.
**Burke was Chief of Naval Operations from 1955 to 1961.

A. K. Murray #2 - 120

we want to talk about Fleet Admiral Leahy.

Commander Murray: Yes, he was one of the five-star people. We painted, of course, all of the five-star people. Admiral Leahy's portrait was painted in the Corcoran too. We did so many there; they were very good to us to let us do that.

Q: Was this while he was still with the Joint Chiefs?

Commander Murray: Yes, he was at that time aide to the President, FDR, when I was doing this. I would like to remark about the remarkable career that man had. He was from a very distinguished class anyway; that was the same class as Hart and Yarnell and Hepburn, I believe.*

Q: It was.

Commander Murray: All of them were on active duty, brought back on, but here comes Admiral Leahy, who had gone to the top being CNO and had also been governor of Puerto Rico and had also been ambassador at Vichy, France, and was now aide to the President. So he had these presidential aiguillettes on, which were quite massive. I mention that

---

*All were in the Naval Academy class of 1897; Admiral Arthur J. Hepburn, USN, served as Commander in Chief, U.S. Fleet in the 1930s.

because the dear fellow insisted on having a martini at lunchtime, and some of our sessions would start in right after lunch. He was quite senior; at that time he was past retirement age but had been put back on the active list.* And he would have a little nap.

Q: At the gallery?

Commander Murray: Yes, while he was sitting there for me. I wanted to try and make the most of what time I had with him, so it was a concrete floor and I would drop a brush on the floor, and it would wake him up. I would turn my back to him and his mouth would fall open, and he would drool all over his uniform and the aiguillettes and everything else. I would take forever to pick the brush up and when I would finally get up he would be finishing mopping himself off with his handkerchief and making the remark, "Gee, I must have dozed off for a moment." This was standard and I tried my best to persuade him not to have his martinis when he was coming in there, but I was so junior to him in rank and everything else that I didn't prevail at all.

At the same time this was going on I was doing Admiral Nimitz's portrait, and both of these paintings were in the

---

*Leahy was born in 1875; he retired as CNO in 1939 at the mandatory retirement age of 64. He was later recalled to active duty, remaining until March 1949, two months before his 74th birthday.

Fleet Admiral William D. Leahy

studio at the same time. One time when he was leaving the room, there was the two easels there, and Admiral Nimitz went by the one of Admiral Leahy, and he stopped and looked at it for a while, and he said, "You know, Al, you've made Bill's nose crooked."

I said, "Yes, I know."

And he said, "Aren't you going to do something about it?"

And I said, "Well, I've done what I can, which is to make it crooked."

And he asked, "What did you do that for?"

"Well it is crooked."

"Oh no," he said, "You take a better look the next time he comes in."

So now comes the next day when I am working with Admiral Nimitz, and no sooner was he in when he said, "You know, a funny thing happened. When I went out on the sidewalk just outside the Corcoran there, I ran into Bill, and I said to him, 'What are you doing, can you come up and have dinner with me?' and he said, 'Sure'. So I had dinner with Bill back in quarters there, and I sat there looking at him and you know, it never dawned on me before until I collided with this painting of yours--his nose *is* four degrees left rudder."

And I thought, "Gee, that's a remarkably salty way to refer to it." So he said, "I asked him what happened."

And Admiral Leahy said, "I lived in a small town, and I liked to play football. We were a little bit rough, and in one of the scrimmages I got my nose broken; it hurt like the dickens, but I could still breathe with it and we didn't have much money in the family and since it functioned I never had anything done to it. So it was always crooked and when I went to the Naval Academy nothing was done with it, and you fellows have known me ever since my late teens and have never seen it any other way, so you thought it was normal and it never even occurred to you that it was bent and out of place like it really is."

Q: It took an artist.

Commander Murray: Yes, to Admiral Nimitz it was normal; it never occurred to him. When you know somebody so well, obvious defects don't exist.

Q: How was he as a subject, other than to fall asleep on you?

Commander Murray: I enjoyed him very much as a subject. He was a rather austere individual in appearance but not that frosty or caustic as you got to know him. But he would be a bit formidable on the first appearance. He had an aide too, who was a humdinger, he managed to sew a

A. K. Murray #2 - 124

button on his coat when it came off there. He had a needle and thread; some aides are really terrific and this one in particular. This happened at the inauguration ceremony for FDR out in front of the Capitol on a cold winter day when they were all out there.* The button came off, and this aide managed to sew the button back on the admiral's coat right while he was sitting there, so I think he ought to get a letter of commendation or something else for that one.

In contrast to some of the others--you were asking what was our objective in the painting. Since so much of Admiral Leahy's achievements were in the top echelon while CNO and then Governor of Puerto Rico and so on, this ought to be quite formal. I had access to a remarkably good chair that Sir William Auckland used to use a lot in portraits, an awfully good English painter that I admire. I was fortunate in using that. It gets a person's elbows in a position that a normal chair won't. The four legs, the rectangle, is turned around so that one leg is between the legs of the sitter, and it allows the arms of the chair to get the elbows in a position that the conventional chair doesn't. This gave me the opportunity to use the gold braid of the fleet admiral and the presidential aiguillettes and so on to its full usefulness in this portrait where I wanted prestige and dignity and high

---
*Franklin D. Roosevelt's last inauguration as President was held at the White House on 20 January 1945.

office to be very much in evidence, which is where Leahy had brought the Navy in these rarefied areas.

I also had the pleasure some time later of going to Boston for the commissioning of the missile frigate Leahy.*

Q: That was after he had died?

Commander Murray: Oh, yes.** It was the first vessel of this type that I had ever seen. It was quite a change for me, having by this time been out of the Navy quite some time and had never seen this type vessel before. The Leahy has since seen rather a distinguished career afloat. As I recall, she is either subject to overhaul or retirement already. Time flies by so. His son was an admiral or was there at the time; this was the first time I had encountered Admiral Leahy's son.***

Q: Now, you are going to turn your attention to Admiral Radford.**** Tell me when you painted him.

Commander Murray: This was after the shooting had stopped. It was painted out in Pearl Harbor when he was CinCPac, and

---

*The USS Leahy (DLG-16) was commissioned 4 August 1962.
**Admiral Leahy died 20 July 1959.
***William H. Leahy retired as a rear admiral in June 1961.
****Admiral Arthur C. Radford, USN, served as Commander in Chief Pacific/Commander in Chief U.S. Pacific Fleet, from 30 April 1949 to 10 July 1953.

Commander of the Trust Territories.* It was a very happy experience or me. We got along very well, and I enjoyed his modesty and reflections on many things. He had been very active in earlier episodes in Hawaii searching for Amelia Earhart when she was down; the square mileage of Pacific Ocean that they searched was incredible, finding of course nothing.** On previous tours in the Pacific he had gotten to know it quite well, but while he was there the 50th anniversary of Samoa occurred as a coaling station for the Navy. So there was a great ceremony down there to which he was invited of course, and he had the kindness to take me along. It was quite an eye-opening event down there with the seaward dances and the whole ceremony, which lasted for about three days.

Admiral Radford was a man who made some remarks that sort of impressed me. Sitting on the beach around lunchtime, he would usually say, "Let's take a fast swim first." I would have lunch in the BOQ, and he would go to his quarters. But first we would drive down to that little beach down by the international airport that the Martin Mariners were using as a runway.*** So we were sitting there on the beach in our bathing suits having a little quick swim before lunch and he said, "How lucky can a

---
*CinCPac--Commander in Chief Pacific.
**Earhart was an American aviatrix who disappeared mysteriously while flying the Pacific Ocean in 1937. The Navy's massive search for her was fruitless.
***Martin Mariners were Navy seaplanes of the era.

Admiral Arthur W. Radford

A. K. Murray #2 - 127

fellow be? Look at me here; look at this blue sky, this wonderful water, this beach, you come to this place; here we are right this minute. I have a four-engine plane. You see that Martin Mariner there; well, I have a four-engine plane at my disposal 24 hours a day. I have a yacht, that barge, that's mine 24 hours a day. I have this limousine, that's 24 hours a day, I have four servants in the house. I get a darn good salary, and I live in this wonderful climate; what is there in industry that can match what I've got?"

I thought, "Well, how nice to have somebody who thinks and savors a little bit of some of the niceties of the top level in professional life in a democracy when you have done well and served your country the best you can and to have these kind of things appreciated and enjoyed as his reference was being clear to me."

One of those days when we were painting down there--I was representing him aboard a carrier as a flying officer, which he was, during an operation presumably during the war in the Pacific where they are executing a turn. I needed a place that would give me a bit of shelter from the elements, so we found a huge door in a warehouse down near the fleet landing that was about as big as a hangar entrance for aircraft, so that's where we were, and I had him in khakis.

Sometimes he would come down--he would be working on

Saturdays and Sundays too the way we did--he might break up a tennis game to come on down and do some posing for me. He would arrive in white shorts for tennis and climb into this gear that I had there, some foul weather oilskin pants. The particular morning I am thinking of, I had killed a lot of centipedes down there in that pile of stuff. He drove up in this little car by himself, jumped out, and with athletic vivacity grabbed hold of those oilskins, dropped his tennis shorts and was about to put his legs down through those and I said, "Hold on a minute, admiral, let's see that there is no centipedes in there."

"Centipedes?"

Gee, he pulled his legs out of there, and I said, "Yes, these spots around here on the floor are the ones I squashed." So, together we turned the things inside out, the legs, and looked over every seam, much like the doughboys did in World War II looking for the lice in the trenches because they all had the lice, right from the commanding general down to the buck private and everybody was looking for the lice because they all had them. So now we are looking for the centipedes, but we only found two. You know some people can get deathly ill from those things.

Q: So you had a makeshift studio there?

Commander Murray: Oh, yes; we had those before. Around

the corner I had the same thing when I was doing Admiral McMorris's portrait when he was commandant out there in Pearl Harbor.* He prided himself on his good nature. He was a remarkably charming man, a very warm fellow.

Q: Wasn't he very heavy too?

Commander Murray: Not too heavy, but he regarded himself as the ugliest man in the Navy, which I don't think was true and certainly not. He was the kindest and the most lovable character that ever came down the road. He was homely as the dickens and he had practically no hair. He had a brilliant strike with cruisers in the Kormandorskis, and that was what I was trying to do in this painting.**

These kona storms that occur in Hawaii are marvelous for many things. I found them useful in doing this thing of McMorris because I wanted him on a bridge scene, presumably in a cruiser up there in the Kormandorskis. The prevailing weather was always terrible up there; it would be overcast, rainy, stormy and gray, so I couldn't have a nice blue Hawaiian sky going on, because that would have lighted up McMorris's head like a simonized fender on a car. His skull reflected the light above it with great

---
*Rear Admiral Charles H. McMorris, USN, Commandant of the 14th Naval District.
**As Commander Task Group 16.6, McMorris commanded a force of two U.S. cruisers and four destroyers in the Battle of the Komandorski Islands, in the Aleutian area, on 26 March 1943.

Rear Admiral Charles H. McMorris

A. K. Murray #2 - 130

accuracy. I needed a gray sky, and the kona storms gave you that, but we hadn't much more than started when the time frame for the storms passed by, and then they weren't going to have any more. So then I was badly distressed for what to do. There was a baseball backstop that was about two stories high down there with chicken wire over this huge frame. I got a tractor and we hauled that around by this warehouse as a windbreak, then I put a tarpaulin up over the two-story high backstop to simulate the gray sky, so that we could work when it wasn't gray. The tarpaulin was high enough up so that it didn't cut off too much light.

The wind got hold of it and we had to use the tractor as a weight to keep it in place, and I got some 2 by 4's to brace it to keep it from roaming around too much, put them down myself. Later that day I got excited running back and forth as I do from the painting to stand back and evaluate what I have done and rushing up to it the next time I fell over the darn thing, put my hand out to break the fall and broke my arm; snapped the end of the radius right off.

Q: Was it your right arm?

Commander Murray: Yes. Well, we were having trouble enough with this gray sky so what we did was to get hold of this mail truck that was surveying duplicate painting materials, easels, and everything else put in there, and requested all the weather stations around Oahu to telephone us if they got overcast skies that looked like they would stay overcast. I wanted to paint McMorris right outdoors in this gray light to make this light convincing for the Aleutians and not something else. He was in foul weather gear, and he had binoculars under his armpit the way a fellow does up on the bridge. And I had two Marines in foul weather gear up on this presumed bridge, too, and we simulated a bulkhead for it with the speaking tube and a pelorus, so it was a convincing scene but all done in Hawaii instead of up in Alaska. We would have that mail truck ready to go like in a fire department. When we got a phone call from some place that was socked in, we would drive up there and start to work. This happened right after I broke my arm and we got this call from the weather station; they thought it was terrific, they thought it was going to be great. We got in the truck, and I did the driving. I thought my arm was going to kill me and he said, "You don't feel very good do you?"

"No, I don't." He didn't offer to drive the truck, and I didn't ask him to. We unloaded and I started to paint again. I said, "I can't handle it; it's killing me."

And he said, "Well, all right, we'll go by Tripler Hospital."

We went by there and I went in and they said, "Oh boy, you sure are fixed up. You are going to stay here with us for quite a while." That's when they found out the thing had broken clean off and reset itself. They didn't put it in a cast, but they kept me in there for six weeks. I had quite a time, and they told me I would never have any more than 40% use of it. In a thing like this you've had it; you'll just have to learn to use the other arm. That floored me, at that age and everything else.

Q: The end of your career?

Commander Murray: So when I got to the therapy, I just overdid everything. The tears would run down my cheeks, but I would stay on for another 10 or 15 minutes doing all these exercises where you are turning and winding up weights and everything else. I think that is what did it, because I've got 100% use of it that I might not have had if I had not made a real determined effort with that therapy.

Q: How soon did it come back?

Commander Murray: Within the six weeks I was back in business and I went back. This was the nice thing with Admiral McMorris. He had a little hut on the other side of the island over near Kaneohe way, and he got that thing all stocked up with groceries and got a car. I could drive it with one hand and gave me the key to that place and said, "Now, you stay over there, and we'll come by and see how you are doing every once in a while."

So I went over there and had a marvelous old time. He kept it stocked up with groceries and everything, and time went by real fast. That's how thoughtful, kind, and sensitive that fellow was--always in a good humor. When we got back, the weather had changed so much, nothing but blue skies all the time and there weren't even any calls from weather stations about being socked in. He said, "All right, now here is what I suggest we do, if it's all right with you." Here is this rear admiral taking to this commander as to what we are going to do, if the commander will permit it.

So he said, "Just before dawn, and that will be around 4:20 at this time, we will have a gray period that will start. It will begin to get light fairly fast, not fast enough that you can't paint, but it is still going to be gray and the zenith won't be blue for probably two hours, maybe more. So I suggest that we meet over there at that fleet landing at 4:30 and I'll have a thermos with some coffee, and some orange juice for breaks that we may have now and then, and we will have about a two-hour period where we can really make some progress. How about it?"

I was all for that. So here was the commandant breaking out over this 4:30 in the morning working out there at just the very break of dawn. Not many fellows would inconvenience themselves to that extent to cooperate, but he did.

Q: You also had made a difficult situation for yourself, trying to recapture Aleutian skies.

Commander Murray: That was the time of his maximum contribution, and with each of these things I was trying to bring that into play where I thought I had a reasonable chance to do it, where it was seemingly appropriate to do, and I felt certainly it was in this case. That was probably the time of his maximum professional contribution that he had spent his whole life getting geared for and waiting for, he had it and he dispatched himself well.

Q: Would you attempt that now, Al, with people in civilian life? You told me about painting a prominent doctor in Chicago. Do you attempt the same type thing?

Commander Murray: Yes, I do. In this case with that doctor for instance--I was studying things yesterday. My technique is to get them here and I take a whole bunch of photos from all directions that I can think of. The process also wears them out a little, which is also what I want. In the broadest generalities, men as a rule, are apt to be on the ground level faster than women. As a model a woman may unconsciously try to create an image for an artist that may not be the real McCoy. A man is more concerned generally with his tonsorial effects and things of that kind; seldom is he putting on a front. It is my job to discover that if it's going on, or try to so that what I am dealing with is the real thing and not be guilty of carrying out some kind of subterfuge of what this fellow really is, or this woman.

In the case this fellow from Chicago, I wanted his biography, which I get from everybody ahead of time. He has had a tremendous life of distinction in the medical way and in the way of service to communities and to the nation on presidential commissions and other things dealing with medicine, He has been selected to head up one of the biggest hospital complexes out there in Chicago, the Rush-Presbyterian complex. It is a combination of three names that I never can pull out of a hat in a hurry. At any rate, it is a huge enterprise. I have him in his white coat, which is the symbol of the professional medical man as against ordinary civilian business clothes. One of the attitudes that we got that I liked--I didn't tell him--I was just watching like a hunter in a blind with these photos that I take. He was looking off a little bit with a contemplative gaze in his eyes, and I am thinking this is probably one of the aspects that I am going to use, because it is the dreamer and the achiever.

He is a fellow who envisions what society may require of medicine in the reasonable future and its capacity to try to meet it and to deliver it, and the difficulty in trying to assemble enthusiastic means to achieve it in today's world with board of directors, trustees, or medical groups and civilian groups. You've got a nasty administrative kind of thing and a collection of support. First of all, you have to dream up where you want to go and what the establishment needs to be and the means to have it and the means to maintain it. So this kind of an aspect of him as the dreamer and the achiever--the way he is looking away and not right at the observer with the head turned the way it is, where there is a look of determination but also there is the dreamer there too. It ties in a little bit of this thing that I am speaking about.

So back to the Navy things--in each of these Navy ones, that is why I am trying to get them in an appropriate mood and role that may be significant to their maximum achievements in their profession.

Q: Had you completed talking about Radford?

Commander Murray: No, not really. In his thoughtfulness

A. K. Murray #2 - 137

here too at one point he said, "You know, this is wonderful country out here that we are in, and one of these days we are going to have a perfectly marvelous day for flying. And when that happens let's not do any painting, and I'll give you a tour of the islands the like of which you will never find any place else. We'll spend all day looking them over."

Q: And he was going to be pilot?

Commander Murray: Yes. So one day he reminded me of this. He said, "You know this is wonderful, we don't get days like this out here very often. You remember what I said about looking these islands over, all of them."

I said, "I sure do, admiral."

He said, "Well, all right; let's do it." He called at Barbers Point and got this Beechcraft available for him and he said, "Let's take the Marine driver with us too." So the three of us went over there and we took off (he didn't have any flight plan), and we are heading now for Kauai, and he called the Black Sands strip to file his flight plan. And the fellow was Army, and he couldn't seem to get the name of the pilot.

He said, "It's Radford."

"I'm sorry. I have the plane number and the flight number. Spell it again." So he spelled it, and the Army fellow said, "No, I don't have it."

So then the admiral says, "Who is the Commander in Chief of the Pacific and the Trust Territories?"

"Admiral Radford," comes the answer.

"Well, that's the pilot."

So we got all that cleared up, and then we landed in a little cow pasture over in Kauai and taxied across that, parked the plane, and went into a drugstore for lunch. It was a terrific experience for me. Flying is what the admiral's whole life has been about, his maximum fun.

Q: Now, you were going to tell me something about Richmond Kelly Turner.

Commander Murray: Admiral Turner was an amphibious commander in World War II, and I was doing this thing of him representing amphibious leadership. I asked him if he would like to have another with him, Admiral Barbey, who was equally distinguished in the amphibious enterprise.* "No," he wanted this a solo operation.

Q: They represented different techniques anyway.

Commander Murray: Well, I think that is the political, professional way to express it.

---

*Rear Admiral Daniel E. Barbey, USN, was the amphibious commander for General Douglas MacArthur's offensive thrust during the Pacific war.

Admiral Richmond K. Turner and staff

I wanted to make these paintings as exciting as I could, and I thought maybe we could use more than one figure as I did with Admiral Spruance and of course with the Nimitz thing; that was the supreme with the surrender scene. At the time I did this, Admiral Turner was the senior naval person at the U.N. He had his Russian counterpart so intimidated that the Russian admiral wouldn't blow his nose without Turner's permission first.

Q: Was Tom Morton with Turner in those days?

Commander Murray: No. Admiral Jim Doyle was his operations officer.* Doyle later on was the prime mover at the Inchon invasion in Korea. Doyle has a son now who is a vice admiral in the CNO's office. I dreamed up a bridge scene to handle the portrait of Turner going back to Guadalcanal days when we had hardly anything to deal with, when we were using Catalinas as dive bombers and everything, since we were not prepared to fight that kind of war. We had so few carriers or anything else as against that wonderful Steichen photo showing 105 carriers in Ulithi and they went clear over the horizon. Going from zero to the maximum things we had was terrific, but in this painting I had envisioned Turner in this AP and his line of columns approaching an amphibious assault.**

---
*Captain James H. Doyle, USN.
**Turner's flagship was the transport McCawley (AP-10).

He is uncovered and instead of a Mae West I used a belt life preserver on him and a Mae West on the others which most everybody was wearing most of the time on shipboard in case of mines or torpedoes or what-have-you, so it was sort of a standard affair. On the scene with him was his operations officer, a Marine officer named Colonel Bucky Harris, and the flag lieutenant Jack Lewis.* They were the four in the scene I was trying to put together in my mind to be Turner's portrait. Turner is standing there in khaki uniform, open neck. His helmet is in his hand with this belt life preserver, and the others are wearing Mae Wests. Coming up a ladder, apparently coming aboard, is Doyle to report to Turner in regard to what is going on. I got some Marines the same size that these fellows were, to put around so I could draw them from life, to make a small-scale composition of this thing. I worked it out to where I felt that we had something that was promising, and then I wanted now to get Turner to come on in and we would start to work on it. He wanted to see what I proposed to do, and I was reluctant to show him, but I had to. In the Navy, I can't do like I can in civilian life where I wouldn't show it to him, so he would have no part of it.

---

*Lieutenant Colonel Harold D. Harris, USMC, staff intelligence officer; Lieutenant Commander John S. Lewis, USN, aide and flag lieutenant.

Q: Why did he object?

Commander Murray: He didn't think it was dramatic enough, so now he told me what he wanted to do. He wanted to have his hand up in the air to indicate that they are steaming in a line of columns. They have no minesweepers; they don't know whether the first ship is going to be blown up or not, and if they stick in this column they assume if this first one doesn't go, then probably this channel in which they are operating in is clear. But there is an impending air assault. (This is his version of it.) This one hand is up and when he drops this hand, that is going to be a signal to the signal officer who is going to tell the fellow at the flaghoist to run up a signal now as they are going to execute a turn to escape the pending air assault. Then he had Doyle get over, "You stand there and you do this, and Lewis you do this, and so on and I am like this." And he is showing it to me. Well I couldn't get very excited about this, and I didn't know quite how to tell him.

I said, "Admiral this is so darn dramatic you can't see you for the action. We've got too much going; we will have to calm this thing down."

Well, I thought he was going to throw the helmet at me. He said, "Get out of here."

So that was the end of that, but I stalled around until Doyle and Lewis came out. I went in and talked with them and they said, "Look, we are with you 100%; we think the old man's off base and we will work on him." I was then doing Kinkaid's portrait in the same studio there at Morgan's where I was going to do this one of Turner, so I was doing his while they were working on Turner. Two weeks went by. Every day they would call me up and give me a progress report; they weren't getting very far, though, with Turner. Finally, after about two weeks they said, "The old man will see you now."

I said, "You mean you have sold him on the idea of the original thing?"

"Yes." So I went over and I said to him in a facetious way--I peeked in the door and said, "I don't have my helmet on, can I come in this way? Am I vulnerable or should I get it?"

He said, "No, I'm not going to attack you. It's all right this way." So I went in and he was very cordial and said, "All right, now when can we start?"

"We can start tomorrow and get going right away with this thing."

Q: Before he changes his mind?

A. K. Murray #2 - 143

Commander Murray: So I went into Doyle's office and I said, "Now fill me in, what in the world happened."

He said, "Well, I'll tell you. We served with him during the major part of the war. We've been with him several years now through combat and the whole works, and here we are back now at the U.N., still with the same boss. What that fellow does, when he doesn't understand something he fights it like mad. It's like getting on a ferris wheel at the county fair. When he has made a 360-degree revolution he has briefed himself on most all of the bugs and problems. Now he begins to understand something about it, so he can deal with it. Now, this ferris wheel has taken him about two weeks. What we did, we went out and bought an amateur's paint set with paints and brushes and bought a little French-type beret. We put a card in it which said, 'To the great fakir. After you have painted your first picture, this will entitle you to kibitz about a subject upon which you know nothing.' That did it."

By this time, he had been filled in and briefed about and shown a lot of the other paintings of this and that and the other thing. So now he was quite willing to go along with anything that we said. At first, when he refused to do this, when he came down to the studio and I laid it all out, I thought he was going to throw that helmet at me. His face clouded all up and he set his mouth in an angry fashion and raised it up, and then Doyle said, "All right, I think we've had enough, we'll adjourn for the day." He was fully aware that the lid was going to fly off any minute. So that first round got nowhere and then's when the time started the two weeks of no results but with Doyle and Lewis working on him.

Q: Was he more placid once you got under way?

Commander Murray: He was completely meek and mild and cooperative then. It was great, but he wore these khaki clothes, as so many of us did. They were starched, and I wanted him topside and under way. This darn starched shirt looked like a cardboard box. I wanted something that would cling to him with the wind blowing on it and things like that, so I got hold of all the electric fans that I could there at the Morgan's house. I had about six of them and had them all aimed at Turner. Things weren't happening worth a darn, so I said, "All right, Admiral, let's take that shirt off and let me see what I can do to crumple it up or something."

He was a little reluctant, but he took it off and there I was looking at this girdle with this canvas strap around here and one up under his armpits, sort of armor plate stitched. It seems he fell down a companionway or something, and he did something to some of the discs in his back and had to use this thing to keep him going. But that wasn't what fouled me up; it was that the shirt was too starched, so I asked him to get those darn things laundered without the starch. Now with the fan, he said, "How much breeze do you want? How many knots do you want?"

And I said, "I didn't know how many knots; I just want the shirt to hang onto your body in a convincing way that would make it look like there is a considerable breeze blowing as there would be at sea when you were topside and under way."

So he said, "Give me my cap." I handed him his cap, and he leaned in front of these fans and he turned around to me and said, "You've got 14 knots here." So we are in this library, and I was roaming around behind the curtain and looking around in the books. And he said, "What are you looking for?"

I said, "I'm looking for a Bible."

"What do you want that for?"

I said, "Well you are so darn sure that's 14 knots, I want to know if you will say it under testimony with the Bible."

"Well, the hell with you," he said. "The reason I know it's 14 knots, this is a real salty cap I have had for a long time. I could never keep the darn thing on if it was one degree over 14 knots, and it is ready to take off right now, that's why I know it's 14 knots of breeze we've got in here."

He gave me a photo of himself afterwards with a most apologetic and charming inscription. He said, "This is offered you in peace for your consideration and patience with an old goat who wasn't about to go along with you, and it turned out to be pretty good after all." I thought it was a very nice breakdown on his part and a warm, friendly gesture.

Q: He was an explosive kind of man anyway, wasn't he?

Commander Murray: Yes, that's why he was quarreling so with Smith out there on Spruance's flagship. But he was a gentle fellow too; he died in his rose garden there in Monterey.* Raymond Spruance, I guess, was the one who found him in the rose garden when he had this heart attack that did him in. Sort of like Ferdinand the Bull, he loved to smell the roses. He can be pretty tough in the bull ring maybe, but he also liked the aroma from a nice rosebud.

---
*Turner died 12 February 1961.

A. K. Murray #3 - 147

Interview Number 3 with Commander Albert K. Murray,
U.S. Naval Reserve (Retired)

Place: Commander Murray's residence in New York City

Date: Monday, 12 January 1981

Interviewer: John T. Mason, Jr.

Q: Why don't we begin by talking about your experiences with Secretary Forrestal?

Commander Murray: Very well. Those were some rather turbulent days. As you know, he was our Secretary of the Navy and came over in that slot as our first Secretary of Defense when the Defense Department was created.*

Q: He was Secretary of Defense when you were painting him?

Commander Murray: Yes, it was not as Secretary of the Navy. The first Secretary of the Navy I painted was John L. Sullivan.** My painting of Forrestal was when he was our first Secretary of Defense, and it was painted over in the dining room in the Pentagon, which faced on the mall entrance with north light. It was reasonably decent kind

---

*James V. Forrestal served as Secretary of the Navy from 19 May 1944 to 17 September 1947. He was Secretary of Defense from 17 September 1947 to 27 March 1949.
**John L. Sullivan served as Secretary of the Navy from 18 September 1947 to 24 May 1949.

Secretary of Defense James V. Forrestal

of light, about the only place in that huge Pentagon where you could function at all. So he made his dining room available; we put a little model stand in there. However, we had a rather stormy time getting started. It seems that he would have no part of anybody wearing a blue suit with gold buttons painting his portrait, and I was then, of course, still active in the Navy.

Q: What was his objection to that?

Commander Murray: He didn't feel that the Navy apparently would have tucked away people in that discipline. But apparently, by that time, I had painted so many and he had been exposed to some of them that he began to change his tune. He had a secretary, a charming red-haired girl named Kate Foley. She had been with him as Secretary of the Navy. Like so many others, she came over with him to the Pentagon in his Defense role, along with his galley and all sorts of other people. Anyway, Kate called me up and said he wanted to talk to me about getting his portrait painted for the Defense Department. I said, "All right, but I have some requirements I would like to talk with him about."

She said, "Don't talk to him about it, put it on a piece of paper. If you talk to him, it goes in one ear and out the other. Put it on paper and you can get somewhere with it." So I wrote it out on paper.

Q: That's a good rule anyway.

Commander Murray: I think so. I came over with it, and there were five items on there. One was that I hoped he would arrange a schedule, which I would keep as a holy command whenever he could make himself available. But I hoped he would have no interruptions when he wanted to set this time.

Q: You mean telephone calls?

Commander Murray: Any kind. There were no telephones in there unless, of course, it was an emergency. In that case, the aides would come in and tell him. He agreed to the whole business, and one by one these things disintegrated. He got a little model stand and put it in the dining room there and got under way. By and by, he said to me, "I have to break one of the rules."

And I said, "What's that?"

He said, "Well, there are two fellows outside that I have to see. Either I'll go out there, or they'll come in here. What do you want to do?"

I didn't want to lose him, so I said, "Ask them to come in here." I liked to paint without the encumbrance of a coat, so I was in my shirtsleeves with my Navy blouse hanging over the back of a chair. In came General Marshall, who was the Secretary of State, and General Eisenhower, who was running SHAEF in Paris.* So they sat down but wouldn't do any talking. Well, with a wave of his hand from the model stand in my direction, Forrestal said, "It's all right, go ahead." They began to talk about the conversion of current weapons to atomic weapons. I had the feeling of the cartoonist's version of the Republican elephant with his ears getting bigger and bigger and sort of flapping in the breeze with the conversation that was going on. This was early in 1947, I believe.

Q: Were you simultaneously studying your subject?

Commander Murray: Sure, I was painting and trying to move this thing along. That was the idea--not to lose him here, because I had to make the best of every opportunity when I could have him in place there. He was a very restless kind of a fellow, and he liked to eat peanuts. And he would be tossing the peanuts up in the air and catching them in his mouth frequently, when he wasn't smoking his pipe. The pipe was simply a device, like Churchill's cigar, I guess. He would very carefully tamp the tobacco into the pipe in a

---

*General of the Army George C. Marshall served as Secretary of State from 1947 to 1949; General of the Army Dwight D. Eisenhower was Army Chief of Staff from November 1945 to February 1948. Eisenhower's role at SHAEF, Supreme Headquarters Allied Expeditionary Force, had ended earlier.

very thoughtful way, but his mind was everywhere else but on the pipe. Then he would sort of contemplate it, and then would put it in his mouth and very ceremoniously light it, two or three matches at a time before the thing would light. And then just after he had a puff of two, he was through with the pipe. He had sort of forgotten and he was not thinking about the pipe, so that's out and now his mind is back again on the things that were on it before he got to the pipe. Suddenly then he would pick it up to light it again and he would go through this whole ritual, and it was usually disgusting to me because he was out of post and it was hard for me to do much, even with his body, because he was moving around so.

On that business of talking in front of me about highly secret stuff, I once asked Tom Gates when he was Secretary of the Navy, "How come everybody talks about everything in front of me at Cabinet level?" I had been painting so many Cabinet members and so on.*

He said, "Don't be so silly, Al, we've got a dossier on you like the New York phone book." Well, everybody seemed to do that, with the exception of Christian Herter when he was Secretary of State.** And he used to go out of the room when he would have something that he would be dealing with, whereas everybody else would discuss it right

---
*Thomas S. Gates, Jr., served as Secretary of the Navy from 1 April 1957 to 7 June 1959.
**Christian A. Herter was Secretary of State, 1959 to 1961.

in front of me.

Mr. Forrestal was a very fascinating man in so many respects. One of the people he brought over from the Navy was a chief petty officer, a marvelous typist and secretary, a stenographer type of fellow, chief yeoman. Forrestal kept voluminous diaries. Every time he would go out at night, on return to the office in the morning, he would dictate to Cutcomb in detail about who was there last night, what they talked about, and his evaluations of the people and of the subjects discussed. Those diaries of Forrestal's were very sought for after his death, because he dealt with so many things in such detail.*

Q: Indeed he did, and apparently they were shocked at the fact that dealt with classified things in a very casual manner.

Commander Murray: I have often thought too that too many things are classified. The classification of things, from my point of view, seems to be--we classify the wrong things too often. Some things that should be classified aren't and vice versa.

Another thing about Forrestal, amusing in my experience--this was his dining room, and it was a great

---

*<u>The Forrestal Diaries</u>, a book edited by Walter Millis, was published by Viking in 1951, two years after Forrestal's suicide.

big room--those rooms there in the Pentagon, like the old Main Navy, were what they called bays. The walls could be easily removed; you could extend them or cut them down. In the building of that building, I think so many government buildings seem to be built where you can put two, three, or four bays together and get a huge room or close them down and get a smaller one. This dining room must have been about four bays; it was enormous.

Q: Similar to hotels in the way they arrange ballrooms and large dining rooms.

Commander Murray: So one day Mr. Forrestal said, "Why don't you come on down for breakfast."

"Thank you very much, what time?"

"Eight o'clock."

"Aye, aye, sir, I'll be here." So at 8:00 o'clock I am in the dining room there and the steward had set the table for two. Mr. Forrestal was often a few minutes late; well, he was about 20 minutes late this time. So he sailed right in, right up to the model stand and sat down like a trained seal going into his act. I forgot to mention this other digression from one of the rules. On the telephone issue--pretty soon a white telephone appeared in there, a little box on the model stand. That was for the White House, the President. Then a black one came in and that one was for all the lesser calls, so now he had a telephone in there. But he also needed to call his aides and do a lot of other things

Q: Did he have a squawk box too?

Commander Murray: No. He did the same thing with a stick with a whole lot of buttons on it. It was a communications thing with wires on it, and each little button would ring the galley or buzz his aides--whichever different aide that he wanted, because there were a lot of them out there--his Marine or Navy aide or secretary or whatever. These buttons were in two rows, and they were only half an inch apart. He got so adept with it--he was a semi-pro boxer and had broken his nose in boxing. He was also in the Lafayette Escadrille from Yale; he had been over in Paris in World War I with the Lafayette Escadrille. Anyway, he got so good with his feet that he could hit the right buzzer without getting out of the model stand chair and ring whomever he wanted, which took a bit of doing. He would have that pretty belly performer's precision with his feet to hit those buttons and not hit the wrong one. He never hit the wrong one; he always hit the right one.

Q: That was an interruption too, because then the aide came rushing in then.

Commander Murray: Yes, but that was better than losing him. These were all defensive things on my part, but they crashed one by one. In this case when we started off, before we got to the button business, he now pushed the button for the steward's mate when the table was set for two. With a wave of his hand at the table setting, he said, "You can take all this away; I had breakfast before I came." So the steward's mate looked at me. Earlier, when I was there a few minutes ahead of time, the steward said, "Don't you want some coffee or something while you are waiting?"

So I thanked him and said, "No, I'll wait."

So I got a look from that steward's mate when the Secretary said this, as much to say, "Well, I offered you something; you missed the boat there." That's what the look said to me. Anyway, it never occurred to Mr. Forrestal that he had forgotten about this. Maybe a week later, he sort of played the same record all over again, "Why don't you come in for breakfast tomorrow?"

"Thank you very much, what time?"

"Eight o'clock."

So this time he was on time. But on that earlier episode, around 9:00 o'clock or 9:30, he said, "I've got to do something out there." I think he was actually going to the bathroom, but anyway he took off and said, "I'll be back in about 20 minutes."

So then I went out in the galley and said, "Okay, if you can rustle up some chow, I certainly would appreciate it," because it was going to be a long haul before noon. So they set up a little table there, and I asked one of the stewards to go out in the dining room as a sentry and let me know when the Secretary came in so I wouldn't hold him up.

Well, they made some bacon and eggs and fixed things up nicely, put a little tablecloth on a little table out there--all this in the galley--and just as I sat down to eat, in comes my sentinel and he said, "The Secretary is outside and wants to know where you are."

So I said, "Just put this stuff back in the oven, and I'll get back out here whenever I can." It turned out I didn't get back there until nearly lunchtime anyhow, and the stuff was vulcanized rubber by then. Forrestal, I don't know how he handled the mess arrangements, because he would set up two or three dates almost for the same thing at the same time. He might call up from the Mayflower Hotel and tell his aide, "I am up here now and am going to have lunch here. We were supposed to have 12 people down there, so you cancel that."--in his dining room, in his office.

So the aide would call up these people and cancel the lunch. This might be about 12:00 o'clock that he gets this call. Maybe about 12:20 or 12:30 he gets another call.

Forrestal is now at the Wardman Park Hotel and tells him, "Put that back on; I am bringing down Senator So-and-So or Such-and-Such; there will be so many of us and we'll be down there in 15 minutes." So now the guy has to rush around and set the thing up again after they threw it all away. This would go on day after day; it would be kind of an on-again-off-again pattern. The guy was very used to this thing and very skillful about it--they were always prepared for this thing to happen, and it was always happening. But I don't know how he ever managed, how those fellows kept their cool and had a decent table in addition.

Q: Did it turn out to be decent?

Commander Murray: Yes, they were quite good at it. But, as I say, it must have been a horrendous mess bill for Forrestal to run the galley in that loose kind of fashion.

Q: What did you try to achieve in your portrait of him?

Commander Murray: I wanted to show the price that he was paying for his job. It was a terribly tough time for Forrestal. It always seemed to me that Stuart Symington had something on Forrestal in a way, because there was an immense amount of deference being shown Symington.* He

---
*W. Stuart Symington was first Secretary of the Air Force, holding office from 18 September 1947 to 24 April 1950.

was then running the Air Force, Secretary of the Air Force. For the chain of command, you go through the old Army way. You would go through the next in command; you don't bypass him. But Symington did; he went directly to the President, right over Forrestal's head. You just don't do that kind of thing. And I often wondered--every time that he would be on the phone, and he was on the phone a great deal while this painting was going on.

Mr. Forrestal would have the thing in one hand for the longest time so that his arm went to sleep and then he would turn it to the other--their conversations were long, long ones. Then he is on the other side, and I was badgered because his head was out of place, and I couldn't see in that kind of light for the painting. And I would have to be filling in other things, so I was acutely aware of these interruptions. I never did discover what the altercations were between the Secretary of Defense and the Secretary of the Air Force that had brought about this kind of situation.

Another thing was Symington was--they were all Democrats at that time--Forrestal was the only Republican in the Cabinet. Then there was another episode. I greatly admire Mr. Truman, and I think the world of him, but he could be pretty crusty at times.* (I never voted for

---

*Harry S Truman was President from 1945 to 1953.

him, but I wish I had.) At one of these sessions, Mr. Forrestal suddenly jumped out of the chair and said, "My God, I forgot all about it, I am supposed to meet the President down at Union Station; I'll see you later." And he took off like a comet right through the door, grabbed his hat, and disappeared. So I went out into the main office there. All his aides came out there; he had a big television set so we flipped it on. All the stations were on this episode; he had that old whistle-stop Pullman with the overhang on the back platform, the real old-time thing that he used for campaigning whistle stops. And that's where he was receiving the Cabinet. There was a red carpet leading from the siding up to the steps to get up on this car.

Q: This was down in Union Station?

Commander Murray: Yes. So the TV cameras were around there, and pretty soon we saw Forrestal galloping down toward those steps on this red carpet. On the back platform was Mr. Truman with his back toward the steps, talking to Carl Vinson, who was facing the steps.* And when he arrived at the bottom of the steps, Mr. Forrestal stopped and waited to be recognized before he climbed the

---

*Representative Carl Vinson (Democrat-Georgia), chairman of the House Armed Services Committee.

steps, and he wasn't. I was disappointed in that, because I think all of us have been in situations where two people are talking and a third arrives. The one whose back is toward that third can see in the face of the one he is talking to an indication that somebody else is there, even if he didn't hear them. There is something in the fact that tells him, and then he would turn around to see what this other fellow was looking at--Vinson, in other words, seeing Forrestal. Furthermore, everybody else in the Cabinet was there, and they had all been accounted for.

Mr. Truman knew darn well who was there and who wasn't; there was only one missing and Vinson apparently had indicated that he was there, but Mr. Truman wouldn't turn around. He was miffed about this. After Mr. Forrestal was on the same level platform on the car, waiting once more to be recognized, just a common courtesy, and he wasn't, so then he turned and walked into the car where all the rest of the Cabinet was. This was one of Mr. Truman's spanking operations that he sometimes indulged in. I often wondered whether he was annoyed because he didn't feel--this is only an assumption on my part--he may have been of the opinion that Mr. Forrestal's contribution to the kitty, as a Republican in this Democratic household, was inappropriate in amount, or something, I don't know.

Q: In the end, he wasn't very fond of him anyway, I think.

Commander Murray: Well, there was that thing, yes. However, I think Mr. Forrestal was a darn good Secretary of Defense, and he had no end of problems and headaches in trying to put that thing together because of the infighting going on. Before that we didn't have any Air Force; it was just the Army and Navy, and there was always enough shoving and pulling and pushing in that way to get all of these professional people to get together to have some semblance of unity in the so-called War Department. Now we put in another one with the Air Force, and each of these fellows vying to help his service as best he can. It was an extremely difficult role to get a smooth-running unified command out of this thing.

Q: How long a period did you work on it?

Commander Murray: It was about four months that we were involved with it, because we were on and off, on and off, but in that time I could see a marked deterioration in Mr. Forrestal. He used to be very prompt in resolving his problems. He seemed to take longer and longer to come to conclusions. So much of the discussion would all be done in my presence there. You could just see a sizable change in the man's mental attitude about things. Then, I guess it was a matter of a month or two after we finished--it was a very short time really-- before he went out the window there.*

Q: Yes, it was right at the end of his career that you got him then.

Commander Murray: He had been so obsessed about the Russians--their whole situation. It bothered his sleep; it bothered him deeply, the whole situation.

Q: Did you ever go out to Prospect Street and paint him out there?

Commander Murray: No, but I was out there to his house. I wanted a fine chair to use in this portrait, a ball-and-claw Chippendale or something like that to put him in. The furniture at the top level in the Pentagon didn't have anything of the elements that I would like to have had, because he was now in a deified role--God being the President and he was probably Gabriel or somebody else of extreme importance in the hierarchy here. And in looking around for one of these chairs, I finally heard that the Forrestals had four Chippendales themselves. So I called Mrs. Forrestal about it to describe it. Would she loan us

---

*During a period of mental depression while a patient at the Bethesda naval hospital, Forrestal killed himself by jumping out a window on 22 May 1949.

one? "Of course, come right out here and see what we have; yes, we have four of them but they have been modified."

She had put some white leather with brass tacks on them. They were quite different really from what they originally were, but they were still Chippendales and good ones. It wasn't what I had in mind at all, so I begged off, but she wouldn't let me beg off. That afternoon I went out when the light began to fail and I couldn't do much more, so I went out there. I had heard about her drinking proclivities, and that was another reason I wasn't too enthusiastic about coming out, but she said, "Come out at about cocktail time." She was sitting in the drawing room with a friend of hers, another woman, and so I asked right away could I see those chairs.

"Oh, no, you have to sit down and have a cocktail."

"Well, thank you very much, Mrs. Forrestal, but I have to get back, time is running out and I have to close up what I am involved with. I just scooted out here for the moment to get a look at those chairs."

"Oh, no, you can't," she said. So I sat down, and she poured me a cocktail. Just as I was about to take a drink, the door opens and here comes Mr. Forrestal. There was a direct vision; he could see right from the front door and the stairs going up. He just waved to me in recognition and he went up the stairs. I thought, "Gee whiz. Here I am in the most awful kind of situation. What am I doing out here having cocktails with his wife?" It embarrassed me no end. He went upstairs and did something or other and pretty soon he came back down. He didn't speak to anybody and went right out. The next day I got a phone call, I was over at Main Navy. There was a fellow named Captain Elder of the Marine Corps; he was the front desk officer there in Mr. Secretary's office.* He called up and said, "You know that Chippendale that you borrowed from Mrs. Forrestal; the front leg is broken off."

I said, "Listen, Elder, this has been a hard day. I'm in no mood for jokes."

"This is no joke; it is sitting right on my table."

I thought, Oh my God, "Well, where's the rest of the chair?"

"It's in the closet."

"Is that all broken up?"

"No, it isn't. The only thing is the front leg and the dowels for the two side pieces, that's on my desk now."

"Okay, I'll be right over." So, I went over and sure enough it was broken. In piecing together what happened, it seemed they have a big rotary brush arrangement that is used for scrubbing and cleaning and polishing the floors in there. It must weigh 200 pounds, electrically driven. That's a red-seal room in there, like so many of those were and you have to have an armed guard with the cleaning

---

*Captain Edward E. Elder, USMC.

forces--highly secret so that nothing gets thrown out and no waste paper basket is accessible to them. So there is this marine armed guard with the fellow who was handling this cleaning thing, and they had Mrs. Forrestal's chair in this coat closet right off the main office there. Apparently that is where they store this scrubber when it wasn't in use.

Some of these cleaning fellows are a little bored with their job, and they sometimes like John Barleycorn to help them out a little bit and relieve fatigue. And that must have been what had happened this night, so the fellow was feeling no pain. And when he opened the door to push the machine in, he just gave it a heave. Along its journey, it bumped into the chair and took it right along until the chair and the machine and the wall arrived simultaneously to the solid obstacle, and off came the front leg. So I asked him if he would call Mrs. Forrestal. He had. So then I called her, and to my astonishment she wasn't at all concerned about it. I was so uncomfortable about calling to tell her about this disaster that I thought she would probably have me drawn and quartered for this. Furthermore, we weren't going to use it anyway; it didn't fit my need.

So she said, "Well, don't be concerned about it, Commander. Downstairs in that building is a marvelous carpenter shop. They can fix anything. Just send it down

A. K. Murray #3 - 166

there; they will fix it."

I thought, Oh my God, those carpenters fixing this thing! It was a museum piece. Then I started calling around to find out where I could get first-class repair, and I called W. and J. Sloane about it, and I asked for the manager of the place. I told him what had happened and what I wanted. He said, "Well, listen, I've been collecting fine furniture all my life, and I've got a marvelous Chippendale, just the thing you are talking about, and I would be delighted if you would use it."

I said, "In view of what happened?"

And he said, "Yes, don't worry."

I asked him, "What about insurance? The government can't insure these things."

"Never mind that, I'll send it over." He was marvelous, so that is what we used. Then he sent me on to some fellow that could really fix this chair up so nobody would ever know. Even Mr. Chippendale would have approved of this repair, for which I was very grateful.

Q: And who stood the cost?

Commander Murray: I don't know. I didn't. It slips me now how it was handled.

Q: Was Forrestal amenable to instruction though?

Commander Murray: Yes, he had a keen wit and humor. One time he said to me, "Who, in your opinion, is the best portrait painter in the world [and after a discreet pause] . . . outside yourself, of course?" But he was maligned so much, the press was always after him. Here are a few little samples--that man was totally dedicated. He was a great American, in my opinion, and had been all the way along--even in his youth when he had volunteered as an aviator in the Lafayette Escadrille, and they were really something in World War I, a real hot outfit. At the time of his funeral (I'm jumping around a bit) I got a telegram inviting me over to Arlington. Arleigh Burke got one; he called me up and said, "I got a telegram; did you get one?"

I said, "Yes."

And he said, "Well, let's go over there together." So he and I went over there together and we sat in the back of this amphitheater and there was only one lone figure behind the caisson carrying his casket, which was John Gingrich in a white uniform.* John and I became great friends, and I was pallbearer for John's funeral later on.

Anyway, after the ceremony was over, Arleigh and I started walking back and we went to the burial place where the remains were put. And there was a small, little

---

*Rear Admiral John E. Gingrich, USN, who, as a captain, had been one of Forrestal's naval aides during World War II.

A. K. Murray #3 - 168

headstone there that said, "James V. Forrestal, Ensign, USNR" and the dates. That was all, it was a little thing about this high. He had been an ensign in the Navy too. He had been a patriotic citizen in a quasi-military function the way you do when your house is on fire, you put it out. Then, he had served with distinction in the Navy, and in the administration end in World War II as Secretary, coming in after Frank Knox, then as our first Secretary of Defense. At that time the partition of Palestine was taking place, and Walter Winchell was hitting below the belt, the way so many of them did to Forrestal.* I don't know why they seemed to pick on him so.

Mr. Truman asked the Secretary for a military version of the partition of Palestine for the creation of Israel--this was in 1947--so Forrestal gave him the military consensus of opinion as to what this all meant and what might be expected. It turned out the net of it seemed to be anti-Zionist, and so Winchell said Forrestal was anti-Jewish and really lit into him. Forrestal gave his boss exactly what he asked for, and it didn't have a darned thing to do with religion or anything else: "This is the way the chips are probably going to be after this thing occurs." So Winchell takes it upon himself to put his meaning in there, and then that creates a whole lot of hullabaloo about it. Winchell was a lieutenant commander

---
*Walter Winchell was a popular syndicated newspaper columnist of the era.

and then a commander in the Naval Reserve.

Q: Winchell was Jewish too, wasn't he?

Commander Murray: Very Jewish. But, in my opinion, some of that vindictive kind of nature that often occurred with the media and which we are getting too much of now. I think the media tries to run things. It seems to me (to digress to the current thing) a little offensive when Barbara Walters and Walter Cronkite come out of Air Force One to meet with Sadat, and he is on a first-name basis.* These people are media people; they are not in the Defense Department or the State Department. And that is the level it should be, and not with the darned communications industry running national policy. I object to them conducting the diplomacy of the nation. I hate to see this kind of thing going on but that, in a sense, was what was occurring with Forrestal and Winchell.

Forrestal was an immensely hard-working man. He had been quite athletic in his youth. He had come in from Wall Street to the Defense Department from Dillon-Read where he had been the number one fellow. He had a lot of friends who were always wanting him to come out and play squash at the Chevy Chase Country Club, or something else, and he

---

*Anwar Sadat served as President of Egypt from 1970 until his assassination in 1981.

A. K. Murray #3 - 170

would always decline. His lights were always on when everybody else had gone home. He would come down there on Saturday and Sunday, and I was always working there on Saturday and Sunday, because I liked to. And who should be down there but Forrestal? And everybody else was somewhere else. The press never commented about this. Now comes the time one Wednesday afternoon after being badgered there, and I got a lot of these calls and Kate Foley was getting them. "For God's sake leave that place and come on out and play squash."

So he said, "All right," and now it's Wednesday at 3:00 o'clock. He is out at Chevy Chase playing squash. The press is out there. They photograph him. "Everybody else in Washington is working like hell, but where is our Secretary of Defense? Playing squash out at Chevy Chase." That burned the stuffing out of me; why didn't they come down on Sunday and look around, or come down on Saturday or at 9:00 o'clock at night any day of the week? No, they'd never do that, but that's where Forrestal was. They catch him the one day maybe in six months when he went out there and now they crucify him. That's the kind of thing that used to get me. But they made his life miserable; there were so darn many of these episodes, every time that they could.

Q: Where did his portrait end? Where is it?

Commander Murray: It is right behind the Secretary of Defense. It has been in a very conspicuous place as our first incumbent in that office, and I think he is generally considered an extremely effective man for that role. It was a very difficult one, to create that thing out of the turmoil that was going on in the military household and the national defense situation, and I think he got that new enterprise off to a darn good start. Apparently that seems to be the general historical feeling as time has gone on to rather establish the fact.

Incidentally, he used to use the word "catastrophic" in a way that (I will digress again a little bit--my father with his four children used to read to us a lot, and he could say words with such meaning that if he used the word "cold"--now today when you and I are talking about such weather as this when it was about 3 degrees above zero this morning, that is really cold--my father would tell us children at bedtime about this "cold" we would have to pull the blankets around us a little bit closer because of the way he said it, it just made you feel cold.) Forrestal had that way of saying about "catastrophe" or "catastrophic." You'd think the end of the world had come, it would be just horrible, and he often used that when he was talking about things in regard to the Soviets. If we aren't careful, we will have a catastrophic situation.

The budget was then running close to 18 billion, and he used the word "catastrophic" there too--18 billion dollars. It seemed to me it was just something; we see the word trillion now and then. Not too long ago, we were seeing billions and that seemed to be a very difficult word to get adjusted to. Millions had lost importance; billions were being referred to and now we are becoming aware of the word "trillion." When we are speaking of an 18 billion budget it was terrifying to Forrestal and look where the darn thing is now--and it isn't so long ago, from 1947 to 1981; it's only a short time. Of course all these other things have come in to push the picture. Forrestal was very cost-conscious and I think, an excellent choice for that job, and that is to Mr. Truman's credit.

Q: Was he pleased with his portrait?

Commander Murray: Yes, I think he was. His wife hated it, though, and she wouldn't even speak to me for some time after that. Forrestal liked it; he had a lot of friends in Newport, and, of course, the Navy was there and always had been in a big way, so he would often go up there and she would be up there too. I had a great many friends in Newport, having painted there considerably before the war, so occasionally I would encounter her at some dinner party, and she would go out of her way never to speak to me. The

A. K. Murray #3 - 173

trouble was she thought that I had shown that he paid too big a price for that job, and I thought that was part of my role in this thing.

Q: In what sense?

Commander Murray: Well, he was sort of a little bit like Atlas; he carried the weight of the world on his shoulders. There was the kind of feeling--"the world is coming apart and what can we do to hold it together? It is almost beyond us but we must do it and we must try."

Q: How was this transposed to canvas?

Commander Murray: It is a kind of concentration. You can almost feel the wheels go round, so to speak, of the mind, of a person who is deeply absorbed in something. It is a difficult thing for me to use words for. Preoccupation isn't the kind of thing either, because that could be with inconsequential things or he could be preoccupied with momentous, serious things. Maybe if I had the painting right in front of me I might be able to point out some things that might seem to stress and point out some of this feeling. It would be a little the bit opposite of what I was saying in regard to Kinkaid and some of the others. I was advised to paint their portraits at a time when the fortunes of war were no longer an urgency. The fighting had stopped and now they are being lionized. The heat is off, and they are very different-looking people than they were when the nation's honor was hanging by a thread.

Q: Enjoying the fruits of their success.

Commander Murray: Yes. It is a very different attitude that is reflected in the face and even in the bearing and all kinds of aspects where it could show up. Forrestal was rather a nervous kind of individual too, and there was a tremendous tenseness. To answer your question in words, I find it rather difficult to come with things that would do it. If we are looking at the painting, I might be able to indicate something.

Q: I suppose the aging process is apparent too?

Commander Murray: Yes, that is always a significant item in it too. Incidentally, that first portrait--I took it over to the Corcoran Gallery, where I had much better working conditions, to check it over when I was about through with it to see if there was anything further that was within my capability to do that might improve it. That studio in the Corcoran is where I had painted so many portraits, Admiral Nimitz and Leahy and a whole batch of others. It was a superb studio. I've never had a better one in my whole professional life, and I've got one of the best in the business right here. But that one in the Corcoran is every bit as good. They have a concrete floor, and there was a great big easel in there that had been used for some huge mural paintings and it had a big crank on it. The crank handle stuck out about a foot.

Well, as I backed across the room, somehow I saw the painting (there is a gadget on these easels that you drop down from the top that hooks into the wood and holds it in place). Somehow that thing on top had not seated properly, and I wasn't aware of it. As I got clear across the room, I saw the canvas falling toward me, and I rushed as fast as I could to get to it, but I didn't quite get there in time. It hit the concrete floor, bounced back and the crank handle went right through the canvas, right through the clavicle--the collar bone--and it was about a four and a half inch rip. I could have cried. I called up Mr. Forrestal and I said, "Now, I hope you are sitting down, I've got some awful news." So I told him, and there was an appalling silence on the other end of the phone.

And then finally he said in this half-way voice, "What do you suggest we do?"

I said, "Well, we have two options, I can get this re-backed and have a repair made that would be pretty good, or we can do it all over again."

There was a long period of appalling silence next; then the voice comes through, not a very robust manner, "What do you suggest we do?"

"Paint another one." There is a longer silence than ever now.

"All right, I'll get some dates together and you can see what you can do, and we'll go at it again." I painted three of them; we had that one re-backed, and that is the one that is still in the Secretary's office. The second one is in the Forrestal Lab in Princeton; it is a slight variation. Then there was one more.

Q: Did he pose for the third one too?

Commander Murray: He posed for all of them and we got extraordinarily good results.

Q: I would think the second and third came easier.

Commander Murray: Yes, I had more of a feel for this thing and I wasn't groping around in the wilderness quite so much as I had been before. I did an interesting thing. Finally, I finished it in the Octagon Room; it is now the American Architectural Association.

Q: Oh yes, at the corner of 18th and New York.

Commander Murray: Just cater corner across from the Corcoran. Up in that room, the Treaty of Ghent was signed in that building.* I was terribly taken with the decor in that room, so I wanted to incorporate some of that to give this a certain elegance that it deserved and needed. A great nation like ours and Defense was such that we hadn't run into the first and only war that we had lost--Vietnam. So that room up there appealed to me a lot. I was always looking around for ways to try to get things to be as significant as I could.

Q: But you didn't get him over there to pose though?

Commander Murray: Yes, but the bulk of it was not done there. We were only in there twice at the tail end, after I had gotten everything well in hand, but it had a nice input. Maybe other things would occur to me about Mr. Forrestal.

Q: Were all those done under the aegis of Combat Art?

Commander Murray: Yes, they were. Naval History finally took us over until I ran into a great jam with Admiral Heffernan, and that was one of the reasons I finally left

---
*The Treaty of Ghent marked the end of the War of 1812.

the Navy.* I couldn't continue to work with him. He was using me for political purposes, and I couldn't function that way. I had one of those red-seal rooms too, and we had some pretty severe altercations. At one time he was going to prefer court-martial charges against me. I suppose I gave him high blood pressure too, but he wanted me to paint certain people that would be important and useful to him in his role, but if we did that we would have to bump some of the others and the time was running out. People were getting older, the war was over, and it didn't seem to me to be the thing to do. If we put on somebody else, we would have to take somebody off, because there wasn't all that time and opportunity.

Then I was accused of insubordination and all sorts of things. That's where John Gingrich comes in again. He ran OP-02 and Heffernan was under OP-02's control, and I couldn't get to first base.** In painting Admiral Radford's portrait out in Hawaii and Admiral McMorris who was represented in the cruisers--he made a grand cruiser strike in the Komandorskis and Alaska--and they were both out in Hawaii. At that time I was doing this painting, Admiral Heffernan showed up. He began to lecture me about what he wanted done with this program, and I tried to explain that I thought if we did that, we were going to

---
*Rear Admiral John B. Heffernan, USN(Ret.), was then director of naval history.
**OP-02 was the Deputy Chief of Naval Operations for Administration.

sacrifice too much of what, in my opinion, we were really targeted for and ought to do, but he wouldn't have any part of that. He got to be very vindicative and caustic and he said, "I'm going to the head. Come on with me and we will discuss this further."

I said, "I'm not going to the head with you. I'll talk to you here if you want me to, but I am not going to the head with you."

And then he said, "I'm going to prefer court-martial charges against you; you can answer in your own way."

So I said, "I think we'll terminate it right now. I'm leaving." So he was Irish promotion rear admiral, and I was only a three-striper, so I took off.* Bill Mott was the legal aide for Admiral Radford, and Bill was a good friend of mine and I told him about it.** I said, "He wants me up there. We are both quartered in BOQ on Makalapa, and he wants me to come in tomorrow at 8:00 o'clock to continue his discussion, but I am not about to do it unless I've got a witness there; he is accusing me of lying and cheating and other things and I find it extremely offensive, and I am not going to take it."

Bill said, "Sure, I'll come over with you." So at 8:00 o'clock, we show up in front of the admiral's door,

---

*Heffernan had been a captain on active duty, then received a "tombstone promotion" to rear admiral at the time of retirement on the basis of combat awards.
**Commander William C. Mott, USN.

and he said, "What's he doing here," meaning Mott.

And I said, "He is a witness."

"Witness for that?"

I said, "For this tirade that I seem to be getting."

"Damn you," he said, "Mott, you get out of here, I'm talking to Murray only."

I said, "Well, we are sticking together here. If you are going to talk to me you are going to talk in front of Mott." He slammed the door. So I went on over to start working with Admiral Radford. We were using a place to paint in down in the fleet landing in a big warehouse in Pearl Harbor. So apparently this had shaken me up so that I was pretty upset, and Admiral Radford said, "Say, you don't feel good, do you?"

I said, "I'm all right."

He said, "Well, you don't act it." So pretty soon he brings it up again, "Is something bothering you?"

I said, "Yes, there is," and just then a car drives up, and it is Heffernan in the sedan. He has come to pay his respects to the Commander in Chief. Radford was then Commander of Pacific Fleet and Trust Territories. So they have quite an exchange and Radford said, "You know, this is a real Navy town--Honolulu--it would be a great idea if we could get all our Combat Art stuff out here in a museum, they have a darn good museum here. Why don't you put that on, I think it would be helpful to the Navy."

"Great idea," says Heffernan.

"So Murray, while you are here, you make arrangements." So I went out to the Honolulu Art Institute, and they were delighted. So now we were to fix a date and everything, and we were going to have this exhibit out there.

Then Heffernan went on back and Radford said, "Do you want to tell me about what was bothering you?"

"No," I said, "we better just forget it." I didn't get into this thing with Admiral Radford, and when we finished the painting and I went back to Washington, being a Scotchman, I wanted to send that stuff out by sea, if we were going to have to do it, and not fly it out there. So I got from the sea command the sailing dates that we would have to meet if we were going to get it out there on the time frame that the museum set up.

So Heffernan said, "For your information we aren't going to have any exhibit out there."

And I said, "Did you notify the people at the institute?"

"No, I didn't, and you're not either."

"Well," I said, "maybe I'm not via Navy channels, but I am going to notify them by MacKay radio, because they are going to be notified." So I took off, and I sent a radiogram out there to both McMorris and Radford to advise them of the fact that due to some circumstances beyond my control here that the program was going to be scrapped and would they make peace with the Art Institute out there. I had sent them a polite dispatch that we found our circumstances made it difficult for us to keep that commitment. Well, the next day Heffernan had a two-page dispatch from Admiral Radford, who was so darn senior to him, ordering him to get that stuff out in toto by the next available transport by air. So all that stuff went down to Patuxent River and went out by air.* He also got a blast from McMorris, both very senior to him.

Of course, he couldn't ignore that by any possible means. So then he sent for me, and I thought he would shoot me on sight, and that's when he locked me out of my room down there. I was in uniform, but I couldn't even get my cap out. The security people all knew me very well, but they wouldn't unlock the door. Since Heffernan had put that seal on the door and stuff, there wasn't anything they could do. So then I had to call up his aide who lived in Bethesda and he had to come in and unlock the door so I could get my cap to put on in order to go home. It was such a stupid and silly kind of thing, but this is the way the thing went.

That's when I went up to see John Nicholas Brown, who was Under Secretary of the Navy at the time and I had known him quite well. I went up to see if I could get myself

---
*Patuxent River Naval Air Station in Maryland.

transferred under some other kind of authority to deal with to close up this program, because I was getting nowhere. I couldn't function anymore with Heffernan on this kind of thing. I had five items there on a piece of paper explaining where my position had been so compromised, and I didn't see how I could get out of it. Brown said he had to go somewhere in one heck of a hurry and was going to be gone for three days and could this wait.

I said, "No it can't, we are in a crisis now."

So he said, "All right," and he called in John Gingrich and said, "This is your baby. You look this thing over and do whatever you think is appropriate." I had known John quite well, and Heffernan worked for Gingrich, so Gingrich said, "I think everything looks all right and what you are asking looks reasonable as far as I can see, so I am going to tell Heffernan he's got to do it. That's all there is to it." He ordered Heffernan to do it, and I thought the poor man would have a stroke or apoplexy. And then that's when I--I never looked at fitness reports all the time I was in the Navy, never even once, but I got a dilly of a fitness report from Heffernan, that's why I never got beyond commander. Anyway, I finally decided this darn place is not for me to continue anymore.

Q: That is a shame, just one . . .

Commander Murray: But we got most of the program completed, and I think it was a very useful one in that it created a lot of good will, which was our main objective. The rank and file of the civilian population that had any affinity for the Navy or who had loved ones in it, or Navy programs that might be broadcast to the nation in general where we would need support from the citizenry for the Navy in the matter of manpower and encouragement for any funds and so on that would be vital to the Navy. And if they had a feeling of trained, responsible leadership in the Navy, which I was trying to do with this portrait group, there would be less foot-dragging, less reluctance on the part of Tom, Dick, and Harry around the country that loved ones that are in the Navy or contemplating being in it and so on, would not be considered cannon fodder and controlled by a lot of crackpots and those negative aspects that were bandied about. But instead, there could be pride and satisfaction in a service that was dedicated to the nation's well-being. So, I think, in that program, we got quite a lot of exposure, which was good too, in those days, particularly. And then it goes down as historical record for whatever that may be useful.

Q: Considerable in the light of this list of things that you did.

A. K. Murray #3 - 185

Commander Murray: We got through quite a lot.

Q: Can we talk about some of the Secretaries of the Navy whom you have painted? John L. Sullivan was one.

Commander Murray: He was the first of the secretaries that I have painted. That was when the flattops were under considerable duress at the time, and I used one of them in this--I try to use whatever I can in these paintings that are significant and pertinent to the time frame in which they are done. At this particular time, the carrier was under considerable assault--the program and so on--so the Secretary was pictured in a room with a fireplace, and over the mantel I put one of these wonderful ship models that the shipbuilders often produced. This one was probably about 36 inches long, or so. I've forgotten whether it was the Saratoga or what.*

Q: A carrier, however.

Commander Murray: Yes, a carrier, in the background. John L. Sullivan was a fellow from New Hampshire, and he was rather cooperative so I made that painting move along. It

---
*The model shown in the painting depicts the intended design of the flush-deck aircraft carrier United States (CVA-58). The keel for the ship was laid 18 April 1949, and construction was terminated five days later by Secretary of Defense Louis A. Johnson. Sullivan resigned in protest.

Secretary of the Navy John L. Sullivan

is always helpful to me when I don't run into the necessity to beg and plead for the time that is needed.

Q: Where is his portrait?

Commander Murray: It is in Combat Art collection or else it's in the Pentagon; at this point I don't know where it is. Some of that stuff has been changed around so that I'm not at all certain where it is right now.

Q: A general question--how many hours do you actually spend on a portrait? How many hours does a man have to pose, in a general sense? I know it depends upon the individuals, but nevertheless.

Commander Murray: Well, these things do vary a great deal. Though I have spent my life at this thing, it seems absurd I can't come up with definitive and accurate numbers, but the darndest things get into the act. For instance, weather has something to do with it in the matter of the drying of the paint. I like to work into a wet ground and when that isn't possible, then I like it to get dried out rather thoroughly and then come on it again. This has to do with the frequency of the sittings and also the type of weather; then sometimes you have to stop right at a time when everything is white hot and going like crazy--just right--and then sometimes you can't continue.

The model has to leave, or some other kind of interruption gets in. Sometimes the model is not in the spirit or mood of the thing, and you then move away from the face and other aspects that you can deal with that need attention. But it may be the time was such that you wanted to pursue with the mood and you are unable to because it wasn't there, or you couldn't get it recreated again. There are so many things that come into play to stretch out the amount of time that is needed. Usually--of course, it depends on how big the canvas is and what sort of background is involved as to how long it is going to take.

Roughly, I would say one-third of the time is spent with the sitter; two-thirds of it is spent in his absence, collecting thoughts, putting things together, experimenting, research and everything else trying to make this thing get off the ground. Once in a while everything, all fits together and once you start it is all there right in front of you. That is ideal, but it doesn't happen too often.

Q: For the most part, there is a lot of frustration. It sounds like an ulcer-creating job.

Commander Murray: Well, it is always disappointing in a

way, because these things can always be better than they are, and you are always trying to do the best you can to make it as good as you can. And you would like it to be everything it ought to be, but as "hope springs eternal in the human breast," you always think that this is the best thing you ever made, and then it doesn't quite turn out that way. There were too many other things that you were groping for, so you are able to start the next one and think this time it's going to work. Well, that's the way it is; it is a very tempting thing, and you are always striving for something better, and that's what makes it fun and exciting, hoping that one day you might make it.

Q: Then there is always the aftermath to contend with. You have spoken about Mrs. Forrestal not speaking to you.

Commander Murray: You get used to those things. I felt I was on good ground and should have done just what I did do or tried to do with that thing. It is unfortunate; you would like to have relationships like existed with Hart, where some 28 years later we had an immensely warm repeat reception, just as we had enjoyed all through his painting. That is the way these things ought to go and hopefully should go. That is where most of your friendships throughout life come from--the people that you had worked with and seem to feel comfortable with what you attempted to do and how you succeeded or went through with it.

Q: Now going back to Mr. Gates; a very personable man, I know him.

Commander Murray: I was very fond of Mr. Gates, the more I got to working with him. He was a most attractive kind of man; he was reluctant to get this done; he always felt that he was not very paintable. He said when anybody takes a picture of him, he always looks like a gangster, to quote him. We were advised to do this in the Pentagon, and again I found a spot right over the mall entrance. Somebody was going to be away for a prolonged absence, and we used his office.

Q: Was he Secretary of the Navy at this point?

Commander Murray: Yes, and Noel Gayler was one of his aides; Draper Kauffman was another one.* One of the nicest things that was ever said to me in my painting career was a compliment made by Noel; he used to come in and look at the painting along toward quitting time, which was when the light was failing in the afternoon. At the end of this thing, he sat there for a while, and he said, "You know, I've been in here each day for a long time

---
*Captain Noel A. M. Gayler, USN; Captain Draper L. Kauffman, USN. Both subsequently became flag officers.

Secretary of the Navy Thomas S. Gates

watching this develop, and I would like to say--of course I am very fond of Tom Gates, as obviously you are. I love that man--but this painting has both an intellect and a soul."

I said, "Well, I never heard anything quite as nice as that; it was the nicest thing anybody could say. If you get a reaction and somebody talks to you that way, I've got something here."

Tom was very cooperative and had a good sense of humor, and I enjoyed working with him very much.

Q: He was somewhat like Forrestal, wasn't he, in that he had a nervous nature?

Commander Murray: No, as his wife said, he is the most unflappable fellow that she could think of, to use a slang expression. I think Forrestal was unflappable too, but I would say Tom Gates was not nearly as uptight--there was a whole lot more slack in the line with Tom than there was with Mr. Forrestal. Tom had been a commander in World War II; he had experience with the fleet, mostly in carriers, although he was not a flying officer.

Q: Gayler said you had succeeded in giving his portrait a soul. Can you describe how you could achieve that? That is an inner being to a man. How do you discern that?

Commander Murray: This again is like your earlier question. It is hard--you need the painting in front of you to be able to point out some of these little things that may suggest it. First of all, it has to be a sensitive observer to read it that way, a very sensitive observer. Many people wouldn't reach this at all. To say that you would handle it this way or that the painter would do it that way and this and that would result; I don't quite know how to answer this kind of thing in words, especially in an abstract way, the way you and I are sitting in this room without having the painting in front of us to consider in the respects that we are asking and talking about.

The painting is a summary of feelings and mood and spirit, the feel of how you react to things. It comes off the brush that way a lot. As so much of Picasso, when we talk this way about it, it comes to mind the way he often plays with the things that he is painting, and he is almost twisting your arm or poking fun at you, taking gross liberties and doing all sorts of provocative things. You would need the painting again to show where these things were occurring and then see if you wouldn't respond to them that way too, especially if they are pointed out; then maybe you could begin to feel some of these things too. A painting is primarily an emotional experience anyway as I see it. It would turn on some of these facets to which you could identify and respond, and then it begins to talk to you the way Noel is referring to.

Q: I take it that basically you have got to like a person you are painting in order to look beneath the surface.

Commander Murray: Oh no, not at all. You can despise the person and get a terrific kind of thing. I did a lawyer one time who came from nowhere and he became immensely successful, and he just defied all social custom because he had arrived in a position where he could have everything his way and just flout custom and get away with it, and because he was an immense success as a trial lawyer. He could talk anybody out of anything, and he knew it. I seized on these characteristics and made the painting as obnoxious as I could, and I thought he would be insulted. I didn't want to make this particular painting but finally got talked into it by a friend who insisted that I do it. You remember a gentleman named McNutt that used to be involved in politics?

Q: Paul V. McNutt of Indiana, yes.*

---

*McNutt was Governor of Indiana in the 1930s, later chairman of the War Manpower Commission during World War II.

Commander Murray: He was a great friend of this fellow, and when he saw the painting he said, "My God, you're not going to--you've seized on every one of his worst characteristics; you are not going to let him have this are you?"

I said, "Sure, this is the way I feel about him."

"Oh," he said, "he's got all those characteristics, but you have put them all right in front and turned the light on them."

And I said, "Well, that's the way I feel about this fellow."

Now, to come into a few specifics, he had a double-breasted suit that he never buttoned up; he's always sort of let the thing hang open. It was a sort of navy blue, but he was a very sharpie sort of Broadway kind of dresser and I had made this thing kind of a purply kind of color, just a little bit on the northern side and I showed some of the gravy from the table he had been sitting to, down the front of his suit, because he didn't ever bother about any of the niceties or anything. He had a double chin that swallowed up his necktie so you couldn't see the knot of his necktie; it was buried somewhere under those chins.

The frontal eminence on his brow--certain people of his ilk had a passage there on the skull that looked like reinforced concrete, and I treated this much in the same kind of way. He had a hard, cruel look in his eye where he could have foreclosed the mortgage on his mother or grandmother and kicked her down the stairs at the same time--with that kind of impunity or lack of sensitivity, cold and ruthless--all of these things I made a sort of clear and emphatic statement on, and that's what bothered McNutt. He recognized that they were there, he felt that it should be soft-pedalled and not put out in the front row.

Q: I can see where you could catch those aspects of a man's character and put them on canvas, but to pursue my original question, in order to see something like soul in an individual, it still seems to me you would have to like a person to see that kind of characteristic?

Commander Murray: Yes you would, you would have to like him very much just as in the other way you detested these characteristics. So, it can work the other way, or a look in the eye that seems to make a man extremely sensitive, or kindly, or compassionate.

Tom had me over to his house a number of times, he had three daughters and one son and he lost the son in a skiing accident when the place burned down in New Hampshire.

Q: That wasn't too many years ago.

Commander Murray: His daughters all adored him, and he them and his wife too. He had done something nice in a fiscal way for one of these girls, and she couldn't get over it, and he just simply dismissed it saying, "Well, that's what dads are for," but in an easy kind of way where he was capable and able to do it. He was full of sympathy, and it was just a nice reflection of that same spirit that he had all the time with people, particularly those who were close to him.

Q: What about Bill Franke?*

Commander Murray: Franke loved the Navy; well, so did Tom. Tom said that was probably the best job he ever had--when he was Secretary of the Navy. He went on, of course, to be Secretary of Defense and then chairman of the board at Morgan Guaranty.

Q: That's where I knew him.

Commander Murray: I did paintings of him in each of those roles, which I was very grateful and happy to do, because I think the world of Tom.

Franke was an accountant, and he came from Vermont.

---
*William B. Franke was Secretary of the Navy from 1959 to 1961 while Gates was Secretary of Defense.

Secretary of the Navy William B. Franke

He was a very interesting kind of fellow, tall and thin, and I did his portrait in a less advantageous area there, right in his office in the Secretary's bay there. He was very cooperative and, as I say, was totally dedicated to the Navy. I had kind of a back door affinity with him and constantly, because one of my best friends in the Navy was Ed Kenney, who was a shipmate on the Boise. He was ship's surgeon and he went on to be Chief of the Bureau of Medicine and Surgery, and when he made the top jump was during Franke's tour.* They were very close and each had a great deal of respect for the other. I think we just lost Franke last year.

Q: Yes. He had great charm.

Commander Murray: Yes, his dedication to the Navy was the strong thing with me. The Navy was paramount in his life; he adored the Navy. So did Tom Gates. Tom told me an interesting thing once. They were in the Mediterranean, and they were going to have liberty and he was going to go to Cairo, which was the nearest big town. Some fellow of Mediterranean ancestry (he may have been a Greek) produced a roll of bills and showed it to Tom--there were very few

---

*Rear Admiral Edward C. Kenney, Medical Corps, USN. After the cruiser Boise (CL-47) returned to the United States for repairs of damage sustained near Guadalcanal in late 1942, Murray painted portraits of a number of the crew members.

of these officers going to go on this liberty so there were few of them to spend it. I think there were probably less than five--and that roll of bills contained over $3,000, and they spent every dime on this liberty, which was only a couple of days. Tom said he had never had such an outing in all his life.

He did an awful lot for the Navy. He used to do all his homework when he would be in hearings in Washington as Secretary. He would get up at 3:00 o'clock in the morning, sometimes at 2:00 and start boning in on everything that he could conceive that they would ask him so that he could give them chapter and verse, right down the line. He would have all his homework right at his fingertips, and he would impress the Congress and the committees.

Q: Personal appearance is important.

Commander Murray: And to deliver the goods while you are doing it. That is where he shone brightly.

Q: You say you also painted him when he was chairman of the Board at Morgan Guaranty. Were the circumstances quite different then and do you have any recollections of that?

Commander Murray: Yes. That was done up here.

A. K. Murray #3 - 198

Q: In his office?

Commander Murray: No, here in this studio. I wanted to keep it in a somewhat modern sense. Tom paints too, in a modern way. He puts it on the floor--doesn't use an easel. He is very much interested in art and does quite nice things too.

Q: Does he do it with a palette or what?

Commander Murray: He uses oil, and watercolor, but mostly oil--at least he did. And then he did some scenes--these were often rather abstract things that he would do. Seldom did anything ever become realistic, but he had a good color sense and a good feel for things. So I wanted to keep this thing as modern as I could and toyed with different kinds of backgrounds and finally started to use a big piece of marble that would give me a variety of colors in abstract shapes that would be appropriate for him and afterward had the opportunity of doing two others down there at the Morgan Bank.

Q: These were done for the bank, or were they done personally?

Commander Murray: They were done for the bank. Anne never

seemed to care much about portraits. That kind of painting seemed not to appeal to her. As a matter of fact, when Tom was thinking of leaving after 12 years in public service-- you see, he had come in before he became Secretary, he had been quite a while in the Navy Department. It seems to me it was something like 12 years.

Q: He was an assistant Secretary.

Commander Murray: Yes. He had been in government service for nearly 12 years, and he was now in the Defense Department, at the time I am speaking of, and he had a little house over there, a nice place, and he was thinking of putting it on the market and going back to civil life. He was concerned with where would he find maximum happiness. He was thinking of getting into the academic world where his father had been (University of Pennsylvania) or going into the financial world. Then Mr. Quarles died.*

The canvas I have used for Tom's portrait was a marvelous old English canvas that I had rolled up saving it for something special and along came that one. So I unrolled it and stretched it out; apparently it had been

---

*Deputy Secretary of Defense Donald Quarles had been slated to move up to replace Neil McElroy as Secretary of Defense. When Quarles died in the spring of 1959, Gates replaced him as Deputy SecDef and then relieved McElroy later the same year as SecDef.

rolled a long time and I usually stretched them very hard. This one apparently I didn't stretch quite as hard as usual so later it developed a few ripples in it, which he called to my attention. On this particular day I came out to his house to look at it. He didn't want it hung there while he was still active, and so temporarily it was hanging in his dining room. So I took it and stretched it and got those ripples out of it and that was the day that Mr. Quarles died. So I said, "Tom, you're going to be Secretary of Defense next, you don't want to sell this house; get it off the market." Well, he thought I was talking through my hat, but he was the natural choice. Who else could slip right into that slot? "You're the admirable solution, just the way the chips lie." And of course that's the way it worked out. So then he became the Secretary of Defense, since the logical number two was no longer available.

Q: And he was there for about a year, I think. It was the end of the Eisenhower Administration.

Commander Murray: Yes, there was another great American. Tom has done a real job, and I think his stewardship while Secretary was awfully good. Also that of Paul Ignatius in the Secretary's role and Charley Thomas and Paul Nitze.*

---
*Paul Ignatius was Secretary of the Navy from 1 September 1967 to 24 January 1969; Charles S. Thomas from 3 May 1954 to 1 April 1957; Paul H. Nitze from 29 November 1963 to 30 June 1967.

Q: Tell me about Nitze, an intellectual type.

Commander Murray: Well, I thought that man had some marvelous opportunities, more perhaps than most people, the roles he had to do in Japan and other things, and then the assault business, and so on. I think he has had some terrific opportunities in the nation's history in recent times--great opportunities. He was a very confident fellow; I enjoyed doing his painting. I saw him last at a dinner party that Jim Holloway had, he and Mrs. Nitze were there. I hadn't seen them for probably 20 years before that, but we picked up again where we left off.

Once, while I was doing Paul Ignatius's portrait he wanted to show it to his daughter who was a young tennis star in her Little League; she was scarcely in her teens. She was going down to Richmond to play in some contest. It was a rainy day and she came in in a yellow slicker--a cute little girl--and she looked at the painting. We were finished with it then, and her father said, "Well, what do you think of it?"

Well, she was embarrassed and kind of reluctant to say anything. Finally she said, "Well, I think it's creepy."

I said, "This is a new kind of word in this youngster's vocabulary. I don't know quite how to evaluate creepy."

Secretary of the Navy Paul H. Nitze

She said, "Well, that's what it is, just creepy." So they filled it in and explained to me that probably it meant that there was so much lightning that it gave her the creeps. At least that's the way they explained it.

Q: That's the interpretation they put on it. Did Ignatius himself appreciate it?

Commander Murray: He seemed to. I did that one too in the Pentagon. That's a hard place to paint in, because its source of light is so low, and you can't illuminate the sitter and the canvas very well. You can't do very big canvases in there either, because you can't get a decent light on it, but those were reasonably small canvases.

Q: But can one deduce from that the fact that the sitter himself isn't attaining as great an importance to it as he should, or else he would make for better facilities and more time?

Commander Murray: The trouble is, down there--well, not necessarily down there; it is anywhere. Painting is hard enough under the best of circumstances and the source of light, if you can get a high source of light, it is usually far better than a lower source of light, it is more

Secretary of the Navy Paul Ignatius

flattering. Most architects make their arrangements with the sun up in the zenith and that overhangs and all projections show up much better in that kind of light. And then you can deal with a canvas, a big one as well as a small one whereas, like in this one we would be handicapped and would have to use a fairly small canvas, because we couldn't get enough light over the people and over the surface of the canvas. And you can't get back away from it. You are right in the model's lap, more or less. You need to make your judgment a bit of distance away to give it carrying power and that sort of thing.

One of the troubles of painting down in Washington in the Defense Department is that you are low man on the totem pole and you are always subject to being bumped and you can't get any kind of continuity. That's why I was trying to get Forrestal to agree to certain rules ahead of time so that we could try at least to get a reasonable opportunity to move the thing along. Otherwise, you are low man on the totem pole, and you are always waiting around for the boss to come, and everybody has access to him except you.

Q: That is what I meant, and I should think that if a man really wants his portrait painted and was sincerely interested in it, that he would make other facilities available.

Commander Murray: Well, somehow they don't. A lot of facilities down there don't exist to my knowledge, and there are only a couple of other studios around town. And the really good one was the Corcoran. I used that to a fare-thee-well.

Q: That is still in being, isn't it?

Commander Murray: No. The Corcoran is, of course, but they have turned that studio and it is now being used for restoration work. They have cut open a window there and they've got ventilating systems.

A. K. Murray #4 - 205

Interview Number 4 with Commander Albert K. Murray,
U.S. Naval Reserve (Retired)

Place: Commander Murray's residence in New York City

Date: Thursday, 28 July 1988

Interviewer: John T. Mason, Jr.

Commander Murray: The landing in southern France was reasonably easy, in my opinion, and some new episodes were involved. Churchill had invented a scheme of putting a bellows on a Sherman tank.* It was like the old Eastman Kodak cameras that had a bellows arrangement you pulled out before you took the pictures.** It would allow about 18 inches of freeboard for that tank to come off of an LST in deep water with a French 75 in it.*** That meant you didn't have to have a DUKW--that's an amphibious truck--to hoist these things out when they got to the beach to give you artillery fire support right away. They provided an addition to what the destroyers had done to breach the anti-tank walls.

At any rate, the walls were reasonably breached, and I soon ran into my boss, Admiral Rodgers.**** He said, "Well, how are you making out? What do you think of it?"

---
*Winston S. Churchill was Prime Minister of Great Britain.
**This was the so-called DD (duplex drive) tank that had propulsion systems for both water and land. The bellows arrangement was made of canvas, and when it was unfolded it displaced enough water so the tank would float.
***LST--tank landing ship; the other reference is to the tank's armament, a 75-millimeter gun.
****Rear Admiral Bertram J. Rodgers, USN, was Commander Task Force 85, which landed the Army's 45th Division at the Bay of Bougnon, in the center of the southern France assault area, on 15 August 1944.

how are you making out? What do you think of it?"

I said, "Well, I think it's a little bit quiet."

He said, "I'll tell you what you do. There's a special service force, the rangers, down there that are trying to get to a fort that's harassing us badly, right in back of Monaco. You go down there and see what you can dig up in a pictorial way. We've lost all contact with those people."

Q: Now, your task at that point was as an artist, was it?

Commander Murray: Yes, I was a combat artist, supposed to cover this thing pictorially as best I could.

When I got to this place, it was between Nice and the casino at Monte Carlo. There's a considerable mountain there called Mont Argil. Halfway up, at a place called Iturbi, was an old Roman town with a Roman aqueduct and a fort. It was a medieval fort with a drawbridge over the moat, which was then all dry, of course. It had a parapet wall with lance windows in there for archers with bows and arrows. It was a real antique.

The rangers had been assigned to get the Germans out of that place. They were harassing our troops because they could look over the parapets right into the town of Monaco. There were 10,000 German troops, and we were not allowed to assault them because that was neutral territory.

Q: Monaco was neutral territory?

Commander Murray: Yes, and if we were apprehended down there in neutral territory, we would be impounded for the rest of the war. So we had to be sure we didn't get down there, and we had to leave the troops alone there. But, finally, these special service guys got the Germans out of there about 3:00 in the afternoon, and we came in.

I discovered that we were at an elevation of 3,000 feet. There was a wonderful view of the whole coast along there, all the way down to Menton on the Italian border and the casino at Monte Carlo and Cape Ferat and all. I'd been sailing around Cape Ferat every night with the PT boats that were sent out to give screening coverage for our fleet of considerable size there--the combatant ships, the support units, and the whole works for the invasion.

Down in front of me, in this afternoon sun in August, was the French cruiser Montcalm having a duel with a 10-inch German cannon in somebody's dry swimming pool on the beach there at Monaco.* While I was observing this thing, it was midafternoon, and the special service crowd hadn't had anything to eat. We had only five gallons of water for a whole company of men. They were trying to get lunch ready, which turned out to be cold beans.

---

*The Montcalm, which was completed in 1937, had a standard displacement of 7,600 tons and was armed with nine 6-inch guns in three triple turrets.

Q: Sounds like a repetition of the loaves and fishes.

Commander Murray: Well, I wasn't interested in lunch, because out here, all of a sudden, I saw a big column of black smoke came up off the fantail of the Montcalm. I thought the German battery had made a direct hit. So I got out my water color business and started making some notes of what I was looking at. The Montcalm sent a signal to two destroyers down there to come up and make a smoke screen cover. She was only about two miles from the beach at the time of this assault and was trying to get into deeper water. It was like sitting on the number-one box in the opera, where you could see the prompter and both sides of the scenery at the same time. You're right up at the proscenium arch there. And that's about where I was, watching this dramatic episode.

These two destroyers responded to the call from the Montcalm, the cruiser under attack. Black smoke was pouring out from these destroyers, and I could see tremendous wakes as they were coming up. They were using all the speed they could get to get up there and surround the Montcalm and give her smoke coverage and hide her from the beach. Well, I was so absorbed in what was going on that I was not aware that I was under observation. When the Germans left Mont Argil, they retired to the summit. It was 5,000 feet at the summit, and we were at 3,000.

They dragged some of their artillery up there, and the first thing that made me aware of them was a tremendous explosion in the courtyard. I hadn't been aware of any of that because I was so absorbed in what I was looking at. Then there was a second explosion. Then there was a third one, and finally it dawned on me that these things were timed. The fourth one that came in veered to the dugout in the fort.

The only other fellow outside with me was a fire control officer from one of the destroyers. Ordinarily, way up there, if that fort needed some artillery support from the beach, we would have to go through the chain of command. Then it would take a little bit of doing before the ship would respond to give us the gunnery support that we wanted. They changed the rules so if you had a fire control officer who had direct radio circuit to the gunnery officer on board the ship, he could get it instantly, what we needed. So they had spotted this German battery up on the summit there, and they wanted fire directed up there, to knock off that attack on us down below. Because these explosions were 88 cannon shells exploding in the courtyard.* Fortunately, their fuzes were a little bit long, so they didn't explode on the fort itself. Then, for some reason or other, the gunnery officer disappeared and

---
*This refers to artillery rounds from German 88-millimeter guns.

went back inside the fort, where everybody else was, getting their lunch ready.

It was hot; it was August. My shirt was open; my helmet was over on the grass, and I was dealing with this water color business. I'd just bought some wonderful water color called bleu verdat. It was a blue-green color that was just right for August weather on the Mediterranean. It was sort of like looking after the kids when the house is on fire, you do some foolish things. I was thinking more about that paint than I was about what was really going on. So I leaned over to get that paint and close up the box. One of these fellows called from that dugout entrance out to the terrace where I was, behind these parapets. I was a two-striper in the Navy, and he yelled over, "For God's sake, Captain, don't you realize you're the target out there?"*

So I leaned over to shut the paint box to get that bleu verdat and then get the hell out of there. Then the next round came; that was five. My dog tags were hanging down from my neck on a chain, and one of the pieces of shrapnel cut a dog tag off. I still have one, but shrapnel got the other one. That's what really alerted me that I was in a hot spot and that I'd better get out of there in a hurry. It was a lucky break.

---

*The collar device for a Navy lieutenant is the same as for an Army captain: two vertical silver bars.

Q: That came pretty close to you.

Commander Murray: That shrapnel that took the dog tag away went right between my chest and my arm. So I got back inside the fort. There was complete silence in there until some voice said, "Well, damn you."

I said, "Well, what's the matter?"

They said, "Well, look at us." They were down on their hands and knees, picking up bean after bean, wiping the dirt and dust off of them from all the debris that the Germans had left in in there when they just left. Nothing happened. They had put some planks up on some empty ammunition boxes to make a little table to put the mess kits on for the beans. But the concussion of these explosions in the moat knocked the table and the ammunition boxes down, and all the beans are now on the floor. But you can't be choosy, so you're going to eat them after you wipe the dirt off. That's what they were all doing. I didn't get any at that time of day because I was the cause of it all. So I'd been spanked by no chow and also having to be apologetic to these guys for putting them in it. If I hadn't been out there, they wouldn't be in the fix they were in right now. I thought, "Well, I'm really lucky being here at all, under the circumstances."

A. K. Murray #4 - 212

Q: There's a second story that pertains to the same area.

Commander Murray: Well, in this assault on southern France, the bulk of it occurred in an area between Sainte-Maxime and Saint-Tropez. The resistance was rather light. We were using PT boats for screening coverage for all the AKs and transports and supply and everything that was needed for this assault.

The Germans had developed what they called a human torpedo. They would take the warhead out of live one and put a little space for an operator to be in there. The propulsion mechanism would be okay. Underneath it they would put a live torpedo. He had about a maximum of 18 inches of freeboard, so he was very low in the water and would be very hard to detect. Radar would have a hard time picking him up. He would leave the beach around 6:00 o'clock or while it was still a little daylight, and then he would hope to maneuver himself out with this torpedo to a firing position on one of the ships.* And they were reasonably effective.**

---

*For details see Captain Robert J. Bulkley, Jr., USNR (Ret.), At Close Quarters: PT Boats in the United States Navy (Washington, D.C.: Naval History Division, 1962), pages 334-337.
**In At Close Quarters Captain Bulkley reports that none of the human torpedoes inflicted any damage in the invasion of southern France.

The Bureau of Ordnance had put out the word, "Get one of those for us. We want to look them over and find out what to do about it." So we'd been practicing a gaffing technique. I'd been fishing in earlier days in my life a little bit, snaring fish, which is about what we were trying to do with this thing. We wanted to snare one of these things with a cable if we could get at it. Well, we would leave the beach over there at Sainte-Maxime around 6:00 o'clock every night and go out for a screening and come back about 10:00 in the morning. In other words, we'd be on a night patrol all night long, trying to give what protection we could from any kind of assaults on these ships that were out there in great numbers.

Well, I'd been on that routine now. I'd be with the Army all day and usually come over and go out with the PT guys at night. That had been going on for two weeks, and I was getting awfully darn tired. These fellows in the boat were always talking about this and that episode with their PT business. And I would say, "Well, why didn't I see any of that?"

"Well, how could you? That was in Guadalcanal." These fellows had just been transferred over to the Atlantic operation from the Pacific. They were a very hot outfit, and they were always recounting episodes of their PT boats, but it was always something somewhere else. So I wrote notebooks full of things that they were telling me,

A. K. Murray #4 - 214

but nothing ever happened where we were.

While this would be going on, the Messerschmitts would come over at 6:00 o'clock every night for an assault on the harbor area, and all the vessels would make smoke. Then the awful din would come when everything that could fire was firing at the Messerschmitts. Then some of them would break away. They'd see our three PT boats coming out to make a screen coverage. They'd just been overhauled, and they could make around 30-33 knots. They were in good shape. Well, what startled me in my introduction to this PT business was that these fellows would stay right on their course, and here came the Messerschmitts. I would think, "Well, gee, are you going to sit here and get mowed down by their machine guns?" Because now we could see the water being spouted by the bullets from the Messerschmitts' firepower as they're approaching us.

They said, "Just keep your shirt on. We know when we're going to have to do it." Right at the last minute, it seemed to me, they sent out a signal from the lead PT boat to make a right turn. Of course, in the water you've got terrific leverage, and you could make practically a right-angle turn. In the air you had to go all the way around Robin Hood's barn to make the same kind of turn. So that would frustrate the Jerries. They'd be mad they missed us. So they'd make a big turn to come back, and they'd try it again. And we'd do the same thing--stay on our course until it seemed to me the next minute or two, if we don't get out of here we'll be blown out of the water. Well, after about three tries the Germans would give up. But this little episode went on every night when we'd go out.

Well, one particular night I wanted to take a nap during the patrol. As I mentioned, I was with the Army all day and then going out with these PT fellows at night, so I had to get some sleep. There was a calm sea, but it was a little bit cold with spray and everything. So I had the Mae West and the flak vest, which was standard equipment. We all had those on, but that wasn't very much protection.*

So I sneaked down to get a nap, down below decks. Well, I wasn't aware of it, but that was verboten. The only one allowed down there was the engineer, and he was only half down there. Because they had run into mines a couple of times, and they lost any personnel that wasn't blown into the sea. You had a much better chance if you were on deck than below. So they dragged me out of there promptly and told me, "Don't ever do that again. Get out of there." But I could not stay awake, and this was before we had that contact. So we were just cruising around looking for something. We had four torpedoes--two on each gunwale. And I got jammed in between the--we had a Bofors

---

*The Mae West was a life jacket worn around the chest. It got its name from a buxom movie actress of the era.

40-millimeter cannon, and I could get wedged in between the torpedo and that and not go overboard and get a little nap. So that's what I was doing.

It was pretty dark. Most of these PT boats, like so many submarines and others would often have a real sharp-eyed kid on board. And one of these fellows thought he saw a likely suspicious target about three miles off the casino there in Cape Ferat. So they talked it over and decided to break the radio silence, and they asked the following boat, "Did you see something suspicious? Can you indicate where it was?"

"Yes, we did." The third boat also thought there was something there. So then we put out flares. They were mounted in rockets to fire them off the PT boat, and also we had aerial flares with phosphorus that would come down on a little parachute and light up the area like Times Square on New Year's Eve--a brilliant light. We tried to sneak in as close to that target as we could and then drop the surface flares, which would have a delayed ignition so that they didn't light up until we had a chance to get back a ways out of the way.

The plan was then to turn around and come in with the flares lighting up the target. Well, the darn things didn't work, so it was all dark down there. But the aerial flares worked. So we came in with only the aerial flares.

We were all madder than hell at whoever was in the factory that had goofed in some way. Now was when we needed those darn things, and they didn't work. This is what happens sometimes in the military when you get mad at the people back home in the factory that allow these sort of things to occur.

Anyway, sure enough, this was one of those human torpedoes. Well, by the grace of God, we snagged that thing. I'm a little ahead of myself because--no, wait a minute. Yes, I am a little bit ahead of myself.

So what happened--they did snag this torpedo, and I'm still asleep. I slept through this whole thing. So when I come to, there's all this commotion on board. Everybody's talking and everything. I got out my notebook again. I said, "Now, is this Guadalcanal again?"

"Guadalcanal? Where the hell have you been?"

They said, "Where's our radar?" So I looked up at the little tower, up above the coxswain there, by our little bridge. It was gone. That had been shot off by cannon. We were under attack from an artillery outfit when this got all lighted up like a Christmas tree, and they blew off the radar.

Now they said, "Now, who's that down there?" It was this blond German kid with this great big black object. That was the torpedo that they snagged on the thing. They had that on board, and they had this kid about 18, scared to death, who was the guy operating the torpedo. So they told me all the story. I was right there, but I didn't see any of this. And I made the water color on this picture from the description that these fellows gave me, having been present but not having seen any of it.

Now, this is a little thing that happened in Main Navy in those days.

Q: The Main Navy in Washington?

Commander Murray: Yeah. It doesn't impinge on anybody's protocol so I guess it's all right to talk about. It has to do with Douglas Fairbanks, Jr., when he was reporting for duty.* I had just finished a portrait of Admiral Hepburn, called Japy Hepburn, who was . . .

Q: Who was he called--Japy?

Commander Murray: Yeah. He was put back on the active list, along with a lot of other very senior flag officers, on the General Board. Now, my assignment had been to paint the General Board's portraits. So I was discussing that issue or something in his office, and his secretary came in and said, "There's a young man out here, Lieutenant Fairbanks, Douglas Fairbanks, reporting to duty."

---

*For Fairbanks's own account of Naval Reserve duty in World War II, see his memoir, <u>A Hell of a War</u> (St. Martin's Press, 1993).

He's to report to my boss, Hepburn. So Hepburn had his feet up on the table in a very easygoing kind of a way. He was an old southern gentleman and old-line Navy. You have to, I guess, have been in the Navy to appreciate the type of fellow this was. He was a salt-of-the-earth kind of a man but very easygoing. "Send him in," says the admiral. So in comes Douglas Fairbanks, who was at the height of box office--extremely handsome. I had been a great Fairbanks fan. His father--<u>Thief of Baghdad</u> and all that.

Q: <u>Mark of Zorro</u>.

Commander Murray: Yeah. And Douglas, Jr. I had great admiration for that whole family, including Mary Pickford. So Hepburn didn't get up. He had one of these tilted-back armchairs with his feet up on the desk. He didn't get up to shake hands or greet him in any kind of a way. He says, "Turn around, young man."

Fairbanks said, "Lieutenant Fairbanks reporting for duty, sir."

And Hepburn didn't say anything except, "Turn around, young man." So Fairbanks questions slightly and turns around.

"All right," says Hepburn to him. As you enter this building, there's a barber shop there. It's run by a fellow named Fuglazy. And as long as I can remember, he's been cutting hair for the Navy."

Q: What's his name?

Commander Murray: Fuglazy. "You go down there and get that G.D. Hollywood ducktail haircut cut off and get it Navy style. He knows how to do it. He's been doing it all his life. Shove off."

Well, I'm appalled at this thing, so Fairbanks was the color of your shirt. He retired out there. I'm a little bit overcome with this whole episode, so I started to take my leave. He says, "Sit down. Stick around." So we shoot the breeze and one thing and another.

By and by, the record is played again. In comes the secretary. She says, "Lieutenant Fairbanks is outside, sir."

He says, "Send him in." So his feet are still up on the desk. So in comes Lieutenant Fairbanks. "All right," he says, "turn around." So he turns around, and the whole recording is repeated again. "There," says Hepburn, "as long as you're wearing that suit, you keep your hair like this, and everything will be just fine. Shove off."

I never could get over that--what must this young man think about this kind of a brusque treatment?

A. K. Murray #4 - 221

Q: But he had been to the barber and got . . .

Commander Murray: He got a Navy haircut.

To my astonishment some, oh, I guess about four or five years ago--I've had the good fortune of being invited umpteen times to the Alfalfa Club dinners in Washington. About four or five years ago, at one of these dinners, during the cocktail period, my old friend Arleigh Burke was over there talking to Fairbanks. He doesn't know anything about this episode I told you about. So I went over to talk to Arleigh, and I didn't know who this was either that was talking to him. After all, it was some 40 years later. But then he said, "Meet Douglas Fairbanks, Jr."

"Oh." So then I reminded him, "I have to tell you a story that you may recall, I think." So then I repeated to him what I've just repeated to you. Well, Fairbanks said it wasn't quite like that. He kind of brushed it off. He didn't want to confess to it, and I never could understand why. And then a little bit later I got ahold of Arleigh, and I said, "I don't understand this. This episode made such an impression on me. I know I was absolutely accurate on what my recollection of that was."

Arleigh said, "Oh, come on, Alex. You know, after all, it's been 40-odd years, and we all get a little bit fuzzy sometimes on some of these details."

I said, "Not this one, Arleigh. This was too darned unusual. I don't forget something like that. But what bothers me is I can't understand is why he wants to avoid it."

Because one other episode in regard to the same man which profoundly impressed me was during the preparation for the southern France operation, Fairbanks was over there at the blockhouse. That's where the planning took place in Naples. And he would wear a British Navy mess jacket. He could get away with things that nobody else could. That same Eisenhower type of--we didn't have that piece of uniform in the American Navy, but the British had it. And Fairbanks--he could put on anything, and it would look like the last word. He was such a handsome guy and had a wonderful figure. And he was wearing this thing.

But what I'm about to say is that when the assault on southern France took place, and we're now in the harbor at Marseille. We're having some trouble getting in there, and there's a small, little island out there that had a German garrison on it that was harassing our troops. The main effort had gone right by this outfit, but they were like jackals biting at your heels and they had to be eliminated. The normal episodes of trying to eliminate them had not been successful. They even brought a cruiser around to polish off the whole island, but they didn't succeed, or the cruiser was needed somewhere else or something. At any rate, so the problem still existed.

Fairbanks dreamed up the idea, let him--he'd take care of that thing, and he did. All he needed was four men. And this whole German garrison over there--it was crazy. "I need a whaleboat--a small boat--and a coxswain and an engineer, and that's all--and an electrician." And he had made some recordings, or got ahold of some, of sounds of a large landing taking place. The clanking of metal and sounds of--he had got ahold of these recordings from someplace--and a broadcasting contraption capable of this. Drawing on his vast movie experience of what you can do with sound effects and everything. So he rigged up this broadcasting arrangement. Your machine here, this recorder, makes me think of it. He got a couple more of these boats in addition, so he deployed these things around. It was a dark night, not a moonlight one, so the obscurity was a little better than it might be on a clear night.

And when the German command heard the sounds of this imminent invasion taking place, they decided they'd already been shot up quite a lot, they'd better throw in the towel. So they surrendered. Not a shot was fired, and the Germans were floored when they saw what had happened. There was nobody there, really, to accept their surrender except

Fairbanks. He got a decoration for that, which he was very deserving.*

Q: He rose to the occasion.

Commander Murray: A little digression about what happened with celebrities in the Navy. Once when I was first starting off down in Florida with this business, my boss was Admiral Kauffman, Reggie Kauffman.** And he was taking me home to dinner one night. The officer candidate school was there. So we were huddled up in the admiral's sedan getting there back to his house one evening when the troops were marching by to chow. And who should be in the last rank of this, on the outside, but Clark Gable--as a buck private but going to officer candidate school. Both the admiral and I were quite impressed and delighted to see him, but Gable was just like everybody else there, coming right in as a buck private at OCS.***

Since you're interested in Hewitt, I'll throw this one in.

Q: Admiral Hewitt, who was in command of the operation in southern France.****

---
*In Fairbanks's account, the purpose of the tactical deception in the area was to tie down troops away from the actual landing site, and in this he succeeded. He does not report capturing any Germans with his force.
**Rear Admiral James R. Kauffman, USN.
***OCS--officer candidate school.
****Vice Admiral H. Kent Hewitt, USN, Commander Eighth Fleet.

Commander Murray: He was my boss in that southern France period. And I was doing a portrait of him in Oran aboard his flagship.* There was a paint detail going up the side. He had five portholes in his quarters there, and I moved him over close to one of the portholes. And this paint detail was describing what had happened, in sailor fashion, on the beach the night before. And they go into the minutest detail. They don't leave out anything. Neither of us had been tuned in on what they were talking about until they--the uniform of the day was a khaki uniform. I'll explain why in a minute.

By and by, while they were hoisting up with this scaffold, they now got level with the porthole. And one of these sailors sticks his head in. It was just big enough to let a human head get through the porthole. And he happened to be right next to where the admiral was sitting. And all he saw were these four stars, apparently, on the collar.** And he yanked his head out so hard that he hit the brass collaring of that porthole and knocked him off the platform they were on. We heard a splash in the water down below. He went overboard when he was on the paint detail coming up the side of the ship.

---

*Hewitt's flagship was the USS Catoctin (AGC-5).
**Hewitt was a three-star admiral at the time, as depicted in Murray's painting.

But that sort of alerted us to the time frame. Suddenly Admiral Hewitt looks and, "Oh, my God," he says, "I'll see you after lunch." He says, "I have a date with a French admiral on the beach." So he takes off in a hurry. There was a clothes tree right near the hatch to go out. He grabs a blouse off the coat tree and a cap.

Pretty soon, I hear a commotion on the quarterdeck through these open portholes. And a voice said, "Out of my way." And so he apparently went down the gangplank, gets into this car, and away he goes. Pretty soon, lunch is over, and back comes the admiral.

He says, "Well, damn you."

I said, "What's the matter, Admiral?"

He said, "Well, why didn't you tell me I was out of uniform?"

"What did you do?"

He said, "Well, look over at that clothes tree. That's a blue blouse. I put that on. There's a black cap cover on that, and I put that cap on. And I'm in a khaki shirt and pants. I should have had a khaki coat and khaki cap cover."

So the French admiral says, "What have you fellows done, changed you uniform regulations again?"

I said, "Oh, that's why I heard a consternation on the quarterdeck. I guess the officer of the deck was trying to tell you you were out of uniform."

He said, "Yes, it was, and I told him to get out of my way because I was late, and I didn't want to hold him up any longer."

[Pause with tape recorder turned off]

Q: This is about what?

Commander Murray: This is about General Vandegrift, A. A. Vandegrift, who was Commandant of the Marine Corps in World War II.*

Q: Is this Guadalcanal or someplace?

Commander Murray: Yes. He got the congressional medal, one of the earlier ones, and also the number-one Marine. And I was to do this portrait, and I thought he'd like to have it in a combat nature because he'd been right in the thick of everything at Guadalcanal and had earned the congressional medal and lived to talk about it, because so many boys were posthumously awarded. But he wanted to be in an administrative capacity, so I was painting it in the Marine Corps headquarters in Washington. And I was having a good deal of trouble at one point with this thing, and he said, "You seem to be having some trouble, don't you?"

---

*General Alexander A. Vandegrift, USMC, was Commandant of the Marine Corps from 1 January 1944 to 31 December 1947.

General Alexander A. Vandegrift

I said, "Yes, I do.'

He said, "Well, what's the matter?"

I said, "Well, a quarter of an inch of measure that I cannot account for in the vertical on your face. And I've been over and over it."

And he said, "I know you have. I've been watching you." But there was a twinkle in his eye.

And I said, "You know something I don't know."

No comment. And then he had two colonels that were his aides, and they were both standing in a little doorway outside his office. And they were amused too. So I wanted this thing to be sober, and not with this facetious attitude that he was showing all the time. So I finally put the brushes down, and I said, "I can't---I've got to sober you up. This isn't going to work with you in this amused state. This is supposed to represent you at a time when the nation's honor is hanging at stake, and you're the Commandant and all that. You can't look like the cat that swallowed the canary."

He said, "All right, I'll tell you what's happened." He said, "You know, I've been having a lot of dental problems. And my dentist says, 'Look, the only way out of this thing is to get an upper and lower denture for you.' So I finally broke down and went ahead and did it. But we've done something about the occlusion, and it is a

A. K. Murray #4 - 229

quarter of an inch different than what it was. That's what your trouble is."

Q: False teeth, and they didn't jibe.

[Pause with tape recorder turned off]

Q: Now you're going to comment on Admiral Sprague. Which Sprague is it?

Commander Murray: Thomas Sprague.*

Q: Thomas Sprague. And this is also Leyte Gulf.

Commander Murray: Well, he had command of the small carriers. I believe his flag was in the White Plains.** I'm not sure of that, but, at any rate, they were rather overwhelmed by a very superior Japanese force. And it was later discovered through a communications failure the Japs withdrew after they had Sprague right by the throat. But, at any rate, the episode I want to speak of was—Sprague was a pretty good sailor man in the matter of canvas and pleasure sailing. He had a chief on board who also was a

---
*Rear Admiral Thomas L. Sprague, commander of an escort carrier task force during the Battle of Leyte Gulf on 25 October 1944.
**Sprague's flagship for the battle was the escort carrier Sangamon (CVE-26). The White Plains (CVE-66) also took part in the battle.

A. K. Murray #4 - 230

darn good sailor.

It happens that one of his carriers had had severe damage in their rudders. They had lost the steering capacity that they needed. They were trying to steer it with the screws on board, but that was a very haphazard, difficult kind of way--there's so much freeboard in a carrier that it can be blown all off the course and everything else without proper steering capability. And the vessel had suffered severe damage in addition. But he's on board, and they're going to bring her back to Mare Island from the Pacific war area where he was, without much steering capability except by the grace of God and the screws on board. Plus they rigged up tarpaulin on the flight deck, maneuvered around with tractors on the flight deck to control the course of the ship. They sailed that ship all . . .

Q: And under escort too, I take it.

Commander Murray: Well, that's beside the point. The thing was, how do you steer this contraption, this big carrier, without normal capabilities, especially when it's vulnerable to wind currents and everything else. But they sailed that thing, with this chief and the admiral employing their sailor experiences in strictly wind-blown vessels. Brought her back all the way underneath the Golden Gate Bridge. And when they got into San Francisco Bay, the Navy wanted them to let them put the tugs on it and take it around. And he would have no part of it until they got up around to get into Mare Island with it.* Then he had to succumb to that. But they had brought that thing back, most of the way across the Pacific, with this Rube Goldberg kind of a method of getting it home, which I thought was a classic for sailor men.**

[Pause with tape recorder turned off]

Commander Murray: This has to do with Holland Smith, a well-publicized officer.

Q: The Marine general.

Commander Murray: Holland was his name, but the press hung one on him, calling him "Howling Mad" Smith.

Q: Yes, they certainly did. They played it to a fare thee well.

---
*Mare Island Navy Yard, Vallejo, California.
**Reuben L. "Rube" Goldberg (1883-1970) was a popular syndicated newspaper cartoonist best known for drawings of mechanical devices that used absurdly unnecessary complexity to achieve simple actions.

Commander Murray: Well, just like they did with Bull Halsey, which was unknown to the family. He was always known as Billy to his family and to his close associates. This Bull Halsey stuff was something invented by the press, and the same with Howling Mad Smith. There were two Smiths. There was an Army Smith and a Marine Smith, and their commands were sometimes confused by the press.

Q: They were not exactly friends, either, were they?

Commander Murray: No. Holland Smith was a pretty selfish kind of a character. One of the things that fascinated me with him was that--an affinity that he enjoyed with his driver and sort of an aide, a sergeant. I was trying to recall his name there this morning. It was either Bradley or Riley; it was an Irish name--one or the other of those. But they had a relationship that was perfectly extraordinary.

It had only one other counterpart in my experience, which was with Captain Moran in the <u>Boise</u> and Eden, the shipfitter.* They were cut out of the same cloth. Moran was a mustang, and Eden was always on report.** He would

---

*Captain Edward J. Moran, USN, commanding officer of the cruiser <u>Boise</u> at Guadalcanal. Seaman First Class Vint Elliott Eden of the ship's damage control party. Both men were the subjects of paintings by Murray.
**A "mustang" is a former enlisted man who becomes an officer. Actually, Moran was a graduate of the class of 1917 at the Naval Academy.

Captain Edward J. Moran

Seaman First Class Vint E. Eden

get into some kind of a ruckus, and so he was always on report. And if for any reason he wasn't on report, Moran at captain's mast would feel he'd been robbed if he couldn't have Eden there to explain what happened, why he got apprehended by the shore patrol or got into trouble and got on report. Because those were exactly the things that Moran used to do, and now he couldn't because he was too senior in rank as an officer but he'd love to. And those two fellows had an affinity that was extraordinary, with a great difference in rank. One was a shipfitter, and the other was a captain of a very distinguished cruiser with a brilliant war record.

But this same kind of an affinity existed between Holland Smith and this driver, Bradley. Each one looked after the other. Nobody said anything, but each had a deep regard for the other and an extraordinary kind of a capability--just like I mentioned in the Boise with Eden, the shipfitter, who also got the Navy Cross in the Cape Esperance Battle. He was no slouch; he was quite a fellow. Those sorts of episodes always intrigued me.

Smith, as I say, was quite a salty kind of a character. I wanted to mention these kinds of two little episodes that happened to him when he was a colonel at Philadelphia Navy Yard. He got into the doghouse of the admiral for some reason or other. He's returning from some mission in Nicaragua, I believe it was. It was wintertime, and he had his greatcoat on. As he approaches the customs, the concrete floor there, it's warm and he's got this greatcoat flung over his arm. And he throws it over the other arm to get some of his papers and credentials out. But he forgot to put down the total of his little entries that he was bringing in. The military had a lot of leeway of stuff you could bring in, but booze was not one of them. And somehow this was overlooked--innocently, I'm sure--but in the process, a flask falls out and breaks on the concrete.

With him is a chaplain in the Marine Corps, a life-long friend. The customs guy looks at the manifest. No brandy on it. It's perfectly obvious what that is on the floor. So here's the culprit, and he's taking in some contraband. Well, the net was that the customs fellow sees this very distinguished officer, and he decides to let it go. He doesn't make an issue out of it at all, so Smith gets in. And as soon as they got out of earshot of the customs fellow, the chaplain says, "Holland, our friendship ceases. We've been friends for 40 years, but it ends now. You took an oath, and I took an oath to support the Constitution of the United States, and you threw it out the window just a minute ago. I'm ashamed of you." Boy, that really cut the old general, right down to the socks.

When he got home, he slammed the door shut and went right upstairs. His wife was telling me about this afterwards. She had dinner ready. He wouldn't eat any dinner. So a little bit later there's a knock on the door, and he hears it. Then he hears the door shut. He can't rest. Oh, incidentally, I forgot to tell you, I've gotten in the doghouse with the admiral in command for something or other. So he didn't have any job for a little while there in the navy yard.

Q: Philadelphia.

Commander Murray: Yeah, just as punishment. So he invented certain things. He put out a bet, which he won, that he could raise a bushel of potatoes on a square foot of dirt. Well, what he did was to put a whole series of things, little trays on that square foot of dirt that had the seeds of the apples on them--potatoes. So he raised a bushel of potatoes on a square foot of dirt. It was sort of stretching things a little bit.

And also, he would keep some chickens, but he didn't like to get out of that bed to feed the chickens in the morning, so invented a little way of--like a funnel, with a--the grain would come down on this inverted funnel and run around a cloth. The chickens could then peck at that stuff. And he had a right-side funnel up above it with a string attached to it that he could pull to let the grain in the top, that would now let the chicken feed into the lower one. And so he could--and he had the string back up to his bedroom. And he could lie in bed and pull the string and feed the chickens.

So he came downstairs then to see what was going on with the front door. And as he goes by the dining room he sees this package. He says, "What's that?" to his wife.

She says, "It's for you. I don't know what it is. Why don't you open it?" So he opens it. He tells his wife. She says, "Why don't you come for dinner?"

He says, "I'm too upset. The chaplain and I had a go-around." And he told her what happened. So then now he wasn't going to eat any dinner, and that's why he shut the door upstairs. But now she says, "There's the package. It looks to me like it's from the chaplain." So he tears the thing open, and, sure enough, in it is a Jager flask, pigskin, with a card from the chaplain. It says, "They assured me in Jager's that if this is dropped on a concrete floor, it will not break."

He said, "Bring on that dinner. I'm hungry as a bear." [Laughter]

Q: Friends after all, huh?

[Pause with tape recorder turned off]

Q: Here's an episode from Martinique?

Commander Murray: Well, no, it's Antigua, where the Navy had a base there. Of course, dawn and sunset surveillance on Martinique, where Admiral Robert had escaped with the carrier Bearn when Vichy France was coming on to the scene.* And we needed to know what was going on. In case she was going to steam out of there, we had to know about it, so we had these patrols that went down there twice a day from Antigua. And the Army had a small air unit there too. They were the only things on Antigua.

But the Coast Guard cutter Campbell was based there for a time. She had a monkey on board, a rhesus type of monkey that would steal items from sailors--your fountain pen or anything they could--and then climb up into the rigging, screeching and making sure you saw where it was all the time. And hold the pen up, or whatever it might be, your glasses case or anything else, and entice you to climb up after it. And it keeps getting higher and higher, and finally it'll get out on some yardarm or something, where you can't quite get out there. Or it's risky if you do. But there was a canvas over the after deck in that hot climate, and the monkey would get out there, hoping you'd do the same. And when it was convinced you weren't going to go any further, it would make a glorious leap off of that like an acrobat in the circus and land on the canvas,

---
*Rear Admiral George Robert, French Navy.

holding on to your pen or whatever. You were always trying to get the item back from the monkey.

But also went on--what brought this conversation up was the dog that somebody found on board the Campbell who could distinguish between a soldier and a sailor--and a Marine. Because they both had khaki uniforms, and they were both wearing khaki shoes. And the only difference that I could find out was the collar devices, and they were both round. And how in the dickens this dog could distinguish between a Marine and a soldier--and it never missed. They were always making bets on it. Any newcomer would say, "That's ridiculous. That dog can't tell." And he would let Marines on board, but he would never let a soldier on board. So they'd take the bets at the gangplank and say, "All right." Of course, everybody puts their money down. They got the Marine, and he gets on board. Now comes the GI, the soldier. Nothing doing. The hair stands up on the back of the neck of the dog. His ears are back, and his teeth are showing. He's not going to let him on board. And he'd never miss. I don't know what kind of a sixth sense that dog had, but that was the fascination in that little base there.

Q: Did you ever have any experience at that Nelson dockyard there.

Commander Murray: Only to examine it, just to see it for the fun of visiting it. That's all. I was always fascinated with the idea--it intrigued me a little bit to read about Nelson's use of it down there in his episodes in the Caribbean.

[Pause with tape recorder turned off]

Commander Murray: We were just talking about attention to details that might seem insignificant to one who is not very observing or intuitive or keenly interested in the thing. I'm speaking now about hands, how important they can be in a portrait. I'm thinking in this particular case about a painting I made of Admiral Sprague, Thomas Sprague, that we commented on about using the canvas on the steering episode of a carrier, to bring her back to the U.S. from the Pacific.

I have him shown on the island, which is the bridge on the carrier, in foul-weather gear to identify the thing that he's standing on, which is the island, and the type of ship. I have him looking aft on the flight deck, where there's a flotilla of aircraft ready for takeoff. But to minimize their importance in the background I've had the ship run through a slight squall, where they're in the fog sort of. They're fading out, which allows me now to concentrate on the admiral. But he's in his environment;

Rear Admiral Thomas L. Sprague

A. K. Murray #4 - 240

he's on board a ship, and the ship obviously is a carrier. And the carrier--they're ready for action. The planes are in a takeoff position, but they're killed in importance by the inclement weather that's currently going on. Sometimes when these operations occur, they've got to take off when the fog breaks. Off they go.

So in regard to the hands, one hand has got a cigarette in it, and it's lighted. That is a--I treated that as a free-wheeling universal joint, so to speak, here of his mind. Where he's anticipating what this new strike is going to be, what they can expect to do, what resistance they might have, what the problems are that are entailed in this strike that's imminent in the painting of this man. This is his command; this is his assignment. This hand represents this planning arrangement. What can I anticipate? What should I do? What will be my options? The other hand has his cap, which is a sou'wester to go with his foul-weather gear. It's wadded up in his fist, hanging on to the bulkhead, the gunwale, the railing there.

That is a--now, both hands run up through the nervous track up--the mind takes care of the hand making the plan. The mind also takes care of the other hand, which is execute. Once the contact is made, this represents the planning of the thing, what we're going to do. Do it. We've got the plan, the business. Which is--and he's gazing off here in this--and under way. I actually had him put in the slipstream of a turned-up prop on a plane in order to get the breeze blowing into his face, where he involuntarily closes his eyes and does these involuntary protective things that nature makes you do when you standing in a stiff breeze.

[Pause with tape recorder turned off]

Q: Now you are doing a portrait which was not military.

Commander Murray: I was discussing here with Jack Mason about details that I attach an importance to, for whatever use it may be to a sensitive person in revealing characteristics of the subject. I mentioned in the case of Admiral Sprague where it tells a story about what the man's duties and job was and how he approaches it. I was discussing one that's here in the studio right now of a civilian but also a Marine sergeant for the assault and reduction of Iwo Jima: David Roderick, who is the CEO of United States Steel Company right now. He's holding his glasses as he takes them down. Just where do we put this? I'm now demonstrating in front of Jack Mason where, at what level do these glasses, do you stop? If it's up here, the sensitive observer can read it, "Do it my way. I told you what to do. Now do it."

That's not a characteristic of the man. He's an open

man. He'll want to listen to the other fellow and think about it: "Maybe it's something I don't agree with, but I think maybe I should agree with it. I want to listen." I don't want this attitude of "Do it my way." Down here, way down--"I'm tired. Can't we sit down?" I don't want that. There is place on here where it's open-minded: "Your treatise is pretty good. I've always believed that white is white. But after reading your treatise, I think it's black." There's an open-mindedness about this position here. He's not prejudiced either way, and he's in tune with what you're saying. He's with it. There's a place to stop this thing on a reading of various kinds of things that a sensitive observer can say, "Is that the way this man thinks? Is this the way he does?" So what the artist then does if he's tuned in the way I am with these kinds of things, you try to think about these things so that you can use them for whatever they may be or not be guilty of overlooking something that you should have thought about.

Q: Yes, and that came out of my observation about what you told me when you were talking about Admiral Zumwalt and painting his portrait, which is a very fine one. And you talked about the difficulty in getting the right angle to his chin, all of which you put in the story, so I don't have to repeat it. But, anyway, that brought on all of this discussion.

Commander Murray: Well, that's why I think these details of this type of nature become pertinent and significant in painting. It isn't just somebody walking in and you pick up the brush and start painting what you're looking at. You need to think about it quite a little bit and try to--especially in this Navy business and wartime experience, to have things as pertinent and as significant as you can.

Q: A question pertaining to that--do you discuss this sort of thing with the subject?

Commander Murray: No. No, I don't because I think it often makes them embarrassed and whatnot. I would ask questions, and the answer would reveal how they feel about it, by asking a left-handed question, to know how his--one can be very self-conscious and awkward in posing for the artist with this thing. And I want to escape that as best I can. And so I caught them on very neutral ground, where they are themselves completely and not--I find that women in particular--and this is speaking in generalities--are much more inclined to put on an act of what they want the artist to see rather than what--I have to separate the wheat from the chaff all time. That's part of my obligation to, just an any biographer would. What I'm doing is writing a biography with paint and a brush, and I just don't want to be a victim of a half-baked performance if I can possibly escape it.

Q: Let's discontinue this, Al, and hopefully have another session?*

Commander Murray: Yes. How long does one of those things run, a couple of hours?

---

*Unfortunately, there were no more sessions to the series.

Air Force, U.S.
   Secretary Stuart Symington received an unusual amount of deference from Secretary of Defense James Forrestal in the late 1940s, 157-158

Aleutian Islands
   Rear Admiral Charles McMorris posed for a Murray portrait after World War II in a setting that simulated the conditions at the Battle of the Komandorski Islands in March 1943, 129-134

Alcohol
   John P. Leeper, assistant director of the Corcoran Art Gallery in Washington, D.C., deliberately spilled beer in Murray's lap while they were having lunch together shortly after World War II, 105-108; Marine Colonel Holland M. Smith got into trouble with a chaplain for smuggling liquor at the Philadelphia Navy Yard in the 1930s, 231-236

Amphibious Warfare
   Amusing incident that Murray remembered occurring on the beach at Salerno during the Army-Navy rehearsals for the invasion of southern France in the summer of 1944, 19-22

Army, U.S.
   Amusing incident that Murray remembered occurring on the beach at Salerno during the Army-Navy rehearsals for the invasion of southern France in the summer of 1944, 19-22; role of Army rangers in the high ground of southern France following the Allied invasion in August 1944, 205-211

Army Air Forces, U.S.
   Overrated its bombing skills in Germany during World War II, 32-33

Art
   See Painting

Barrow, General Robert H., USMC
   Marine Corps Commandant who demonstrated interest in Murray's portrait painting techniques, 41-42

Brown, John Nicholas
   As Under Secretary of the Navy in the early 1950s, turned to Rear Admiral John Gingrich to settle a dispute between Murray and Rear Admiral John Heffernan, 182-183

Burke, Admiral Arleigh A., USN (USNA, 1923)
Description of the operations of his Destroyer Squadron 23 in the Solomon Islands during World War II, 111-114; personality, 114-116; description of the pose Murray used in painting his portrait, 116-118; reaction to being passed over initially in the late 1940s for promotion to flag rank, 118-119; met with Murray at an Alfalfa Club dinner and talked about actor Douglas Fairbanks, Jr., 221-222

Campbell, USCGC (WPG-32)
Coast Guard cutter that had a mischievous monkey on board when operating in the Caribbean early in World War II, 237-238

Catoctin, USS (AGC-5)
Flagship for Vice Admiral Kent Hewitt, Commander Eighth Fleet in 1944, 224-227

Chapman, General Leonard F., USMC
Marine Corps Commandant who was extremely cooperative with Murray in sitting for his portrait in the late 1960s, 57

Coast Guard, U.S.
The cutter Campbell (WPG-32) had a mischievous monkey on board when operating in the Caribbean early in World War II, 237-238

Corcoran Gallery, Washington, D.C.
Provided a studio in which Murray painted a number of portraits of naval personnel during and shortly after World War II, 62, 104-108, 120, 174-175, 204

Cutcomb, Chief Yeoman Jack E., USN
Remarkable enlisted man who had an uncanny ability to take dictation while working for Secretary of Defense James Forrestal in the late 1940s, 82-84, 152

Destroyer Squadron 23
Description of the operations under Captain Arleigh Burke in the Solomon Islands during World War II, 111-114

Doyle, Captain James H., USN (USNA, 1920)
Operations officer for Vice Admiral Richmond K. Turner during World War II, he later helped persuade Turner to go along with Murray's ideas concerning his portrait, 139-144

Eden, Seaman First Class Vint E.
Sailor who frequently got into trouble while serving in the cruiser Boise (CL-47) during World War II, 232-233

Elder, Captain Edward E., USMC
 As aide to Secretary of Defense James Forrestal, he notified Murray when a chair belonging to Forrestal was accidentally broken in the late 1940s, 164-166

Fairbanks, Lieutenant Commander Douglas E., Jr.
 Actor who reported for active naval service in World War II with hair too long for Navy standards, 218-222; performance in tactical deception operations during the invasion of southern France in the summer of 1944, 222-224

Foley, Catherine Starr
 Served as personal secretary to James Forrestal when he was Secretary of the Navy and Secretary of Defense in the 1940s, 82-83, 148

Fonda, Henry
 Actor who interceded to get Fleet Admiral William Halsey a ticket to the Broadway play <u>Mister Roberts</u> in the late 1940s, 30-31

Forrestal, James V.
 As Secretary of Defense in the late 1940s, he had an eccentric style for dictating correspondence, 82-84; difficulties involved when Murray painted his portrait, 147-167, 174-176; personal habits, including absentmindedness, 150-151, 153-157; showed considerable deference to Secretary of the Air Force Stuart Symington, 157-158; received a rude snub from President Harry Truman at the railroad station in Washington, D.C., 158-160; performance as Secretary of Defense, 161, 171-172; deterioration in mental condition, 161-162; funeral in 1949, 167-168; attacked by prominent newspaper columnist Walter Winchell, 168-170; Mrs. Forrestal didn't like the portrait Murray did of her husband, 172-173; Forrestal's portrait reflects the difficulties of his job, 172-174

France
 Amusing incident that Murray remembered occurring on the beach at Salerno during the Army-Navy rehearsals for the invasion of southern France in the summer of 1944, 19-22; Murray's experiences during the invasion of southern France in August 1944, 205-218

Franke, William B.
 Secretary of the Navy, 1959-61, whose portrait Murray painted, 195-196

French Navy
   The cruiser Montcalm had a duel with a German shore battery following the invasion of southern France in August 1944, 207-208; the carrier Bearn holed up for safety in Martinique early in World War II, 237

Gates, Thomas S.
   Individual who served as Secretary of the Navy and Secretary of Defense in the 1950s, evaluated by Murray as extremely intelligent, 31; had no hesitation about discussing sensitive matters in front of Murray when his portrait was being painted, 151; Murray's painting of him as Secretary of the Navy, 189-192, 199-200; calm personality, 190, 194-195; dedication to Navy, 196-197; portrait done when Gates was with Morgan Guaranty, 197-199

Gayler, Captain Noel A. M., USN (USNA, 1935)
   As aide to Secretary of the Navy Thomas Gates, commented favorably on Murray's portrait of Gates, 189-192

General Board
   Murray painted portraits of various members of the board during World War II: Admiral Thomas Hart, 59-65; Admiral Harry Yarnell, 63-65; Rear Admiral Edward C. Kalbfus, 65-74; Admiral Arthur J. Hepburn, 218-222

German Army
   Fired artillery shells on Allied positions in southern France following the invasion in August 1944, 206-211

German Navy
   Used a manned torpedo in some operations in the Mediterranean in World War II, 212-218

Gingrich, Rear Admiral John E., USN (USNA, 1920)
   Former aide to Secretary of Defense James Forrestal, he was involved in Forrestal's funeral in 1949; helped Murray in a squabble with the head of naval history in the early 1950s, 178, 183

Gunfire--Naval
   The French cruiser Montcalm had a duel with a German shore battery following the invasion of southern France in August 1944, 207-208

Halsey, Mrs. Frances
   The wife of the famous admiral was an inveterate talker, 12; hoodwinked Admiral Ernest King into signing orders for a friend of the Halseys, 12-16

Halsey, Fleet Admiral William F., Jr., USN (USNA, 1904)
Role as a fund-raiser for the University of Virginia after World War II, 3-4; role in the Battle of Leyte Gulf in October 1944, 5-6; Murray brought up the Battle of Leyte Gulf to get Halsey into the right frame of mind for his portrait, 8-11; Halsey's wife hoodwinked Admiral Ernest King into signing orders for a friend of the Halseys, 12-16; temperament, 28-29, 40-41; views during World War II about the Japanese as enemies, 29-30; actor Henry Fonda interceded to get Halsey a ticket to the Broadway play <u>Mister Roberts</u> in the late 1940s, 30-31; intelligence, 31-32; description of the setting of Murray's portrait of him, 33-35, 46; had an arresting physical appearance, 35-36, 95; orders to Captain Arleigh Burke in the Solomon Islands in 1943, 111

Hart, Admiral Thomas C., USN (USNA, 1897)
Description of the pose Murray captured while painting this member of the General Board during World War II, 59-63; served Murray a very potent drink in his apartment, 63-65; role in getting Rear Admiral Edward Kalbfus to cease criticizing Murray's portrait of him, 71-74; warm relationship with Murray, 188

Harvey, Brenda
Harvey's Bristol Cream heiress into whose dress Murray tossed a coin during a party shortly before World War II, 67-69

Hawaiian Islands
Admiral Arthur Radford served as his own pilot one day in the early 1950s when he took Murray out for a flight around Hawaii, 136-138

Heffernan, Rear Admiral John B., USN (Ret.) (USNA, 1917)
As head of naval history in the 1950s, he created difficulties for Murray because of their differing priorities concerning people to be painted, 177-183

Hepburn, Admiral Arthur J., USN (Ret.) (USNA, 1897)
As a member of the Navy's General Board early in World War II heckled actor Douglas Fairbanks, Jr., for having hair too long for Navy standards, 218-222

Herter, Christian
Secretary of State who used to leave the room to discuss sensitive matters rather than share them with Murray, 151-152

Hewitt, Vice Admiral H. Kent, USN (USNA, 1907)
   As Eighth Fleet commander in 1944, inadvertently put on the wrong hat while leaving a portrait sitting with Murray, 224-22[?]

Holloway, Admiral James L. III, USN (USMC, 1943)
   As Chief of Naval Operations in the mid-1970s, he demonstrated interest in Murray's portrait painting techniques, 41-42, 44, 109

Ignatius, Paul
   Secretary of the Navy in the late 1960s, his portrait by Murray drew an unfavorable review from his daughter, 201-202

Ingram, Vice Admiral Jonas J., USN (USNA, 1907)
   As Commander South Atlantic Force during World War II, his command was involved in antisubmarine warfare, 16-17; got paint on his uniform while on an inspection tour of a ship, 18-19

Italy
   Amusing incident that Murray remembered occurring on the beach at Salerno during the Army-Navy rehearsals for the invasion of southern France in the summer of 1944, 19-22

Japanese Navy
   Operations against Captain Arleigh Burke's Destroyer Squadron 23 in the Solomon Islands in 1943, 111-114

Kalbfus, Rear Admiral Edward C., USN (Ret.) (USNA, 1899)
   Member of the General Board who was displeased with Murray's portrait of him, painted during World War II, until his friends started teasing him about it, 65-74

Kalbfus, Mrs. Syria Brown
   Took a condescending attitude toward Murray and had a negative reaction to his portrait of her husband, which was painted during World War II, 66-70

King, Fleet Admiral Ernest J., USN (USNA, 1901)
   When he was chosen as Chief of Naval Operations early in World War II, announced he was the resident SOB, 2, 99-100; his personality was a mixture of sensitivity and toughness, 2-3, 99-100; Admiral William Halsey's wife hoodwinked King into signing orders for a friend of the Halseys, 12-16; provided a houseboat for the use of Commander South Atlantic Force, Vice Admiral Jonas Ingram, during World War II, 16-18; pose used for portrait painted by Murray, 94-97; agreed to pose for Murray in 1945 because he knew the war was about to end, 97-99; was partially incapacitated by a stroke after World War II, 100-102

Kinkaid, Admiral Thomas C., USN (USNA, 1908)
Received a report from Rear Admiral Jesse Oldendorf after the Battle of Surigao Strait in October 1944, 7-8; his perspective on the Battle of Leyte Gulf differed considerably from Admiral Halsey's, 10, 24-25; became greatly disturbed when Murray brought up the Leyte Gulf episode while doing his portrait, 24-28; once Murray got him into the right mood for a portrait, it was easy to recapture, 43-45; setting for Murray's portrait of him was a shipboard scene, 45-46

Komandorski Islands, Battle of
Rear Admiral Charles McMorris posed for a Murray portrait after World War II in a setting that simulated the conditions at the battle in March 1943, 129-134

Lawrence, Charles
Art curator who was a model for a telephone talker in Murray's painting of Admiral Arleigh Burke, 117-119

Leahy, Fleet Admiral William D., USN (USNA, 1897)
Summary of his long and remarkable career, 120-121; not always alert during posing sessions with Murray, 121; Admiral Chester Nimitz's remark about Leahy's nose appearing off-center in his portrait, 121-123; had a top-notch aide, 123-124; special chair used in the portrait, 124-125

Leeper, John P.
As assistant director of the Corcoran Art Gallery in Washington, D.C., he deliberately spilled beer in Murray's lap while they were having lunch together shortly after World War II, 105-108

Lewis, Lieutenant Commander John S., USN (USNA, 1932)
Served as flag lieutenant to Vice Admiral Richmond K. Turner during World War II, later helped convince Turner to go along with Murray's ideas for a painting, 140-144

Leyte Gulf, Battle of
Admiral William F. Halsey and Vice Admiral Thomas Kinkaid had controversial roles in this battle fought in October 1944, 5-6, 10-11, 24-25, 28, 32; Rear Admiral Jesse B. Oldendorf reported on the battle to Admiral Kinkaid, 7-8

Lovette, Captain Leland P., USN (USNA, 1918)
Navy public information director who was present when a portrait of Rear Admiral Edward Kalbfus was being shown to the General Board during World War II, 71-73

MacArthur, General of the Army Douglas (USMA, 1903)
   As depicted in various paintings, 104, 109

McMorris, Vice Admiral Charles H., USN (USNA, 1912)
   Posed for Murray portrait after World War II in a setting that simulated the conditions at the Battle of the Komandorski Islands in March 1943, 129-134; personality, 133-134

Medical Problems
   Fleet Admiral Ernest J. King was partially incapacitated by a stroke following World War II, 100-102; observation on constipation problems among old-time submariners, 109-110; Murray broke his arm while doing some paintings in Hawaii following World War II, 131-133

Military Academy, U.S., West Point, New York
   Portrait gallery appeared to honor the Corps of Engineers, for the most part, rather than combat arms, 109

Missouri, USS (BB-63)
   Battleship that served as the setting for Murray's portrait of Fleet Admiral Chester Nimitz, 103-105, 108

Mister Roberts
   Broadway stage play for which actor Henry Fonda interceded to get a ticket for Fleet Admiral William Halsey in the late 1940s, 30-31

Mitscher, Vice Admiral Marc A., USN (USNA, 1910)
   Frustrated by Admiral William Halsey's action during the Battle of Leyte Gulf in October 1944, 5-6; Murray's perception of Mitscher's approach to warfare, 28-29, 32

Montcalm (French cruiser)
   Had a duel with a German shore battery following the invasion of southern France in August 1944, 207-208

Moran, Captain Edward J., USN (USNA, 1917)
   As commanding officer of the light cruiser Boise (CL-47) during World War II, had to administer discipline frequently to Seaman Vint Eden, 232-233

Morgan, Captain Junius, USNR
   Son the famous financier J. P. Morgan, he provided Murray a studio to use for his painting while in New York City in the 1940s, 23-24

Mott, Commander William C., USN (USNA, 1933)
   Became involved in a squabble between Murray and Rear Admiral John Heffernan in the early 1950s, 179-180

Murray, Commander Albert K., USNR (Ret.)
   As an artist, he was perceptive about the personal characteristics of people, 2, 46-49, 80-82, 134-136; used various techniques to get subjects into the right frame of mind for portrait sittings, 8-11, 24-28, 43-45, 58; Murray's techniques for emphasizing certain aspects of a portrait, 41-42, 49-53, 95-97, 241-244; received a very potent drink in the apartment of Admiral Thomas Hart during World War II, 63-65; broke his arm while doing some paintings in Hawaii following World War II, 131-133; Secretary of Defense James Forrestal was initially skeptical about being painted by Murray because he was in the Navy, 148; difficulties in dealing with Rear Admiral John Heffernan, director of naval history, in the early 1950s, 177-183; physical and psychological aspects of creating a painting, 186-187; experiences during the invasion of southern France in August 1944, 205-218

News Media
   Reporters for the wire services used guesswork when sending in dispatches about the Battle of Surigao Strait in October 1944, 7-8

New York Naval Shipyard
   Admiral Thomas Kinkaid lived in fine quarters in the yard while serving as Commander Eastern Sea Frontier in the late 1940s, 25-28

Nimitz, Fleet Admiral Chester W., USN (USNA, 1905)
   Pleasant, modest, thoughtful man who served as Commander in Chief Pacific Fleet during World War II, 74-79; Murray's portrait of him was set on board the battleship Missouri (BB-63), 103-105, 108; observations on primitive conditions on board early submarines, 109-111; remark about Admiral William Leahy's nose appearing off-center in his portrait, 121-123

O'Kane, Commander Richard H., USN (USNA, 1934)
   World War II submarine skipper who could be either aggressive or compassionate, as the situation dictated, 114-115

Oldendorf, Rear Admiral Jesse B., USN (USNA, 1909)
   Was irritated when talking with newsmen before reporting to Vice Admiral Thomas Kinkaid about the Battle of Surigao Strait in October 1944, 7-8

PT Boats
Provided screening coverage for Allied forces during the invasion of southern France in August 1944, 212-218

Painting
As an artist, Murray was perceptive about the personal characteristics of people, 2, 40-41. 46-49, 80-82, 134-136; the Navy's post-World War II art program included portraits of the five-star admirals, representatives of various ship types, and enlisted personnel, 4-5; Murray used various techniques to get subjects into the right frame of mind for portrait sittings, 8-11, 24-28, 43-45, 58; description of the setting of Murray's portrait of Admiral William F. Halsey, 33-35, 46; reasons for depicting Admiral Elmo Zumwalt in a particular way, 36-40; Murray's techniques for emphasizing certain aspects of a portrait, 41-42, 49-53, 95-97, 191-194, 241-244; description of the shipboard setting for Admiral Thomas Kinkaid's portrait, 45-46; pose used in Murray's painting of Admiral Thomas Hart, 59-63; portrait of Harry Yarnell, 61; Rear Admiral Kalbfus was displeased with Murray's painting of him until his friends started teasing him about it, 65-74; Murray painted Vice Admiral Raymond Spruance with members of his staff, 93-94; pose for portrait of Fleet Admiral Ernest J. King, 94-97; Murray's portrait of Fleet Admiral Chester Nimitz was set on board the battleship <u>Missouri</u> (BB-63), 103-105, 108; setting and pose for Murray's painting of Admiral Arleigh Burke, 116-118; painting of the portrait of Fleet Admiral William Leahy, 121-125; Murray's sessions for the portrait of Admiral Arthur Radford, 125-128; Rear Admiral Charles McMorris posed for a Murray portrait after World War II in a setting that simulated the conditions at the Battle of the Komandorski Islands in March 1943, 129-134; Admiral Richmond K. Turner was quite strong-willed in trying to dictate how Murray would portray him in his painting, 138-146; difficulties involved in painting the portrait of Secretary of Defense James Forrestal in the late 1940s, 147-167, 174-176; benefits of Murray's work for the Navy art program, 184; painting of Secretary of the Navy John L. Sullivan, 185-186; physical and psychological aspects of creating a painting, 186-187; portrait of Secretary of the Navy Thomas Gates, 189-192, 194-195; portraits of Secretary of the Navy William Franke, 195-200; portrait of Secretary of the Navy Paul Ignatius, 201-202; Murray's experiences as a combat artist during the invasion of southern France in August 1944, 205-218; Murray had a difficult time with the portrait of Marine Commandant A. A. Vandegrift because of the general's dental work, 227-229; setting for the portrait of Rear Admiral Thomas L. Sprague was a carrier, 239-241; portrait of U.S. Steel CEO David Roderick, 241-242

Pentagon, Arlington, Virginia
A dining room served as an impromptu art studio when Murray was painting the portrait of Secretary of Defense James Forrestal in the late 1940s, 147-149, 152-153; light sources make it a difficult place in which to paint, 202-203

Radford, Admiral Arthur W., USN (USNA, 1916)
Posed for Murray while serving as Commander in Chief Pacific in the early 1950s, 125-128; setting and pose for the painting, 127-128; served as his own pilot one day when he took Murray out for a flight around Hawaii, 136-138; arranged for an exhibit of Navy art in Hawaii in the early 1950s, 180-181

Rodgers, Rear Admiral Bertram J., USN (USNA, 1916)
Arranged for Murray to do artwork ashore during the invasion of southern France in August 1944, 205-206

Salerno, Italy
Amusing incident that Murray remembered occurring on the beach at Salerno during the Army-Navy rehearsals for the invasion of southern France in the summer of 1944, 19-22

Smith, Lieutenant General Holland M., USMC
Relationship with Vice Admiral Raymond Spruance during the Marianas campaign in the spring of 1944, 92-93; got into trouble with a chaplain for smuggling liquor when he was a colonel at the Philadelphia Navy Yard in the 1930s, 231-236

Soviet Union
Role in getting in at the end of the Pacific war in 1945, after Japan was essentially defeated, 98-99

Sprague, Rear Admiral Thomas L., USN (USNA, 1918)
One of his escort carriers was rigged with a sail during World War II when the ship suffered rudder damage, 229-231; setting for Murray's portrait was on board a carrier, 239-241

Spruance, Admiral Raymond A., USN (USNA, 1907)
Evaluated by Murray as being extremely intelligent, 31; modest and self-effacing personality, 84, 87, 91-92; working style as president of the Naval War College in the late 1940s, 84-85; liked to walk and swim for exercise, 85-87; taste in beverages, 87-89; behavior toward his pet dog, 89-91; relationship with subordinate commanders in the Fifth Fleet during World War II, 92-93; Murray painted him with other members of his staff in the portrait, 93-94; found the body of Admiral Richmond K. Turner when he died in 1961, 146

Submariners
Fleet Admiral Chester Nimitz observed that old-time submariners suffered from constipation problems because of the primitive toilets on board the boats, 109-110; used sections of newspaper as insulation in poorly heated boats, 110-111

Sullivan, John L.
Secretary of the Navy whose portrait by Murray includes a model of an aircraft carrier, 185-186

Symington, W. Stuart
As Air Force Secretary in the late 1940s, he received an unusual amount of deference from Secretary of Defense James Forrestal, 157-158

Torpedoes
The German Navy used a manned torpedo in some operations in the Mediterranean in World War II, 212-218

Truman, President Harry S
Rudely snubbed Secretary of Defense James Forrestal in an incident at the railroad station in Washington, D.C., in the late 1940s, 158-160

Turner, Admiral Richmond K., USN (USNA, 1908)
Relationship with Vice Admiral Raymond Spruance during the Marianas campaign in the spring of 1944, 92-93; was quite strong-willed in trying to dictate how Murray would portray him in his painting, done shortly after World War II, 138-146

Uniforms--Naval
While inspecting a destroyer in his role as Commander South Atlantic Force during World War II, Vice Admiral Jonas Ingram got gray paint on a brand-new uniform, 18-19; Vice Admiral Kent Hewitt inadvertently wore the wrong cap for his uniform when he went to have lunch with a French admiral in 1944, 224-227

Vandegrift, General Alexander A., USMC
Marine Commandant whose portrait Murray painted in the mid-1940s, difficult because of dental work, 227-229

Virginia, University of
Fleet Admiral William F. Halsey, who attended the university before going to the Naval Academy, served as a fund-raiser in the years following World War II, 3-4

Weather
   In doing a painting of Rear Admiral Charles McMorris after World War II, Murray wanted stormy skies around Hawaii to duplicate conditions in the Aleutian Islands, 129-134

Whistler, James
   Noted artist who was arrogant in dealing with people whose portraits he painted, 59

Winchell, Walter
   Prominent newspaper columnist who attacked Secretary of Defense James Forrestal in the late 1940s, 168-170

Yarnell, Admiral Harry E., USN (USNA, 1897)
   Murray painted a full-length portrait of this officer who commanded the U.S. Asiatic Fleet in the late 1930s, 61; visited Admiral Thomas Hart's apartment when Hart served Murray a very potent drink on one occasion during World War II, 63-65

Zumwalt, Admiral Elmo R., Jr., USN (USNA, 1943)
   Description of the facial expression and pose Murray captured while painting this Chief of Naval Operations in the early 1970s, 36-40, 49-51; personal characteristics, 54-56, 58-59